THE CELLULOID PERSUASION

MOVIES AND THE LIBERAL ARTS

by

Lawrence L. Murray

WILLIAM B. EERDMANS PUBLISHING COMPANY
GRAND RAPIDS, MICHIGAN

Library of Congress Cataloging in Publication Data

Murray, Lawrence L.
    The celluloid persuasion.

    Bibliography: p. 147.
    1. History—Study and teaching (Higher)—United States—
Audio-visual aids.   2. Moving-pictures in higher education—
United States.   I. Title.
D16.255.A8M87   378.1'7'33523   79-16764
ISBN 0-8028-1813-7

For
Chris, Julie, and Tim

CONTENTS

ACKNOWLEDGMENTS

As A YOUNG professor of history in the early seventies, I was rudely confronted by shrinking enrollments in my chosen discipline. My future in academia seemed bleak indeed; survival was uppermost in my mind. Years of graduate training in the intricacies of historical research offered no guidelines for attracting prodigal students. Casting about for something that would solve my problems and insure tenure, I hit upon the idea of bringing movies into the classroom. I had heard that others had tried the technique, with apparent success.

The gimmick worked remarkably well in filling empty seats. Pedagogically, the results were varied, and colleagues' opinions were dubious. More importantly, I had trouble sustaining enrollments in the ensuing semesters. The simple problem was that I had not fully thought through just what I was doing. With no more foundation to go on than hearsay, my methodology was one of trial and error. Eventually I did develop a workable approach, but I learned that others were paralleling my erratic performance. Each of us was "reinventing the wheel." The purpose of this book is to break the needless cycle of duplication, to acquaint the uninitiated with the practical fundamentals while at the same time pursuing questions of theory and value.

In my struggle to formulate a methodology for teaching history with film, I have had the benefit of the assistance and criticism of many individuals. Two of them stand out: Dr. Carol A. Hyland and Dr. David E. Meerse, former colleagues at the State University of New York at Fredonia. When I suggested pooling our physical and intellectual resources in a cooperative venture, they enthusiastically agreed. My conversion to the celluloid persuasion might have degenerated into apostasy without their assistance and encouragement, and this book would never have been written.

INTRODUCTION

THE IDEA OF using Hollywood movies in the classroom is only about a decade old. Other filmic forms such as documentaries and instructional productions have a longer heritage. Yet all three types share in a common tradition: their introduction into the academic world was greeted by contradictory and often heated responses, and their climb to respectability has been thorny. Some view the academic use of celluloid as the pedagogical hallmark of a modern, media-oriented era; others see it as an invidious intrusion of a bastardized kind of entertainment-oriented instruction. At times the antagonists have been shrill in their praise and denunciation, but there is finally evidence of détente.

Speaking before the 1977 meeting of the Popular Culture Association of America, Professor Stuart Samuels announced that the legitimacy and acceptance of commercial feature films in the history curriculum was beyond question. To bolster his argument, he referred to the growing number of books and articles about film, the granting of graduate degrees and research fellowships, and the number of sessions at professional meetings devoted to movies. The University of Pennsylvania historian spiritedly concluded that the interdisciplinary study of history and film had achieved a secure niche in higher education, that its practitioners were no longer iconoclasts but were in the mainstream.

Though elated with the transition from neglect to popularity, Samuels was upset that methodological considerations had received so little attention in the rush to study film. His analysis—consciously or unconsciously—ignored teaching situations in its focus on research activity. This neglect seemed to say that the methodological situation in teaching with film was so bad that there were no useful illustrations of the sound classroom use of film. The failure to formulate substantial methodological superstructures, he thought, was generating intellectual chaos. Shoddy technique had superseded mature reflection, threatening that hard-won legitimacy and acceptance. He concluded that the educational role and function of film had reached a crucial juncture and that the future was cloudy.

Less histrionic, Mr. David Sohn, coordinator for the Evanston, Illinois school system and associate editor of *Media and Methods,* has expressed greater confidence in the acceptance and legitimacy as well as popularity of films of all types in the classroom. Focusing attention upon English at the secondary level, Sohn has claimed that movies "are simply an overwhelming presence that won't disappear." More importantly, the roar and excitement about film in the classroom has diminished because it "has settled in as a part of the school environment and achieved dignity and acceptance as part of the curriculum." He sees no difficulty with methodology, partly because of his own extensive work and partly because of the steady stream of suggestions offered in his journal.

Yet, like Samuels, Sohn does think that the future of instruction based on the visual media in the secondary schools is in danger. Reduced funding is threatening the enthusiasm for film study of all types, and the culprit is the federal government. Sohn believes that the availability of federal moneys since 1965 was in large measure responsible for prompting instructors to try various forms of the celluloid persuasion, but that the reduction of those appropriations is strangling creative impulses. In the wake of the

"Proposition Thirteen mentality," his fears would be more pronounced. The rallying cry of "back to the basics," a perennial imponderable which has intensified, is yet another factor that may undermine resources for multimedia approaches.

The opinions of Samuels and Sohn are frequently repeated by other educators, humanists, and social scientists. They have an unquestionable validity. The explosive popularity of audiovisual instruction in the wake of Marshall McLuhan's dictum that "the medium is the message" has caused as many problems as it has solved. Teachers often did not understand what McLuhan meant any more than their predecessors comprehended John Dewey's call for "learning by doing." But the race was on to replace chalk with celluloid. Movie projectors and other machines were brought into the classroom, and, from all appearances, Johnny still cannot read. The public becomes more and more confused and angry, as the situation in the schools continues to deteriorate. Their worst fears appear confirmed—that their children are being entertained rather than educated with all of these audiovisual apparati.

While recognizing the phenomenal expansion of film in instructional settings, I hesitate to generalize too quickly or too broadly on that fact. To confuse popularity with endorsement is to mistake toleration for acceptance. More teachers than ever are booking films, and movies are finding their way into other educational institutions such as libraries, museums, and galleries. Those involved, however, are a distinct minority and essentially a youthful one. Even Sohn, after claiming "the dignity of acceptance," admitted that an "uncomfortably large" group of teachers and administrators remain skeptical if not hostile. Critics think filmic presentations are supplementary at best, useless at worst, and diversionary under any circumstances. Frequently, acceptance indicates toleration and not legitimacy. That is especially true in the case of Hollywood features.

My own observations and experiences lead me to conclusions more guarded than those of Samuels and Sohn. A balance exists between the supporters of film and their opponents, with toleration functioning as an intermediary position between legitimacy and condemnation. Which way the pendulum will swing depends upon the capacity of teachers to solve the two major problems identified by Samuels and Sohn—methodology and budget. Those twin dilemmas reflect a larger set of circumstances that imperil the utility of film as a pedagogical tool. They are also code words that stand for more than superficial definitions might reveal.

The term "methodology" raises a number of related issues that have not been fully addressed by the proponents of films. Methodology obviously implies a discussion of how to use movies. However, I think that it would be a mistake to begin there, for it overlooks the more fundamental question of why. The facile assumption that because ours is a media-responsive society teachers should employ the visual media in their instruction is wholly inadequate. Many methodological quandaries would disappear if teachers were to completely understand and conceptualize why they bring movies into the classroom. Before worrying about how they are going to teach with movies, instructors must first determine what they expect to accomplish with them. In addition, they must ask whether film will help to better achieve those goals or whether they can be reached equally well through more traditional means. In short, teachers must determine if film provides a unique opportunity. Why and how are two interwoven questions: answers to the latter logically follow from those to the former.

The word "budget" also takes us into a larger arena, the technical aspects of utilizing movies. Funding determines whether one even uses movies, for an inadequate amount will undermine the best methods. It will invariably affect how one uses film and to a lesser degree why. But budget is only the first of a series of technical hurdles that must be cleared. The novice must learn a variety of new techniques: how to order pictures, proper scheduling, and the intricacies of the 16-millimeter projector and video playback machines, for example. A breakdown anywhere between allocating a budget and final screening can destroy the process. A teacher with lecture in hand can survive the absence of chalk, but his mechanized counterpart cannot overcome a burned-out projector bulb. Along with developing a methodology, he must sharpen his mechanical expertise.

I intend to examine and analyze the use of films in the liberal arts curriculum, organizing my arguments around the twin prongs of methodology and budget. Within the methodological realm, the focus will be on commercial feature productions. I will also offer some commentary concerning instructional films, documentaries (usually more accurately identified as compilation films), and television. Of the three, television will receive more attention because of its role in conveying feature pictures and because of its attempts to emulate Hollywood with its made-for-TV movies and mini-series. I do not view television as a medium distinct from the movies in the sense that the electronic medium of radio and the print media of books, magazines, and newspapers are. The products of the movies and television are virtually identical; it is only the means of transmission that differs. However, that difference can at times be significant, and I will address it when it arises. Instructional and documentary films, in addition to television, should also be recognized as distinct entities that deserve individual attention beyond what is possible here. The methods and operating principles used for the movies do not always apply to other media forms, and teaching methodologies are not ordinarily interchangeable.

Of necessity, I plan to offer some of my perspectives on the place of the movies in twentieth-century life. A historical survey of an evolving medium provides a context for understanding why one would want to use movies in the classroom. A symbiotic relationship exists between the movies and society: art imitates life and life imitates art. I will attempt to reveal some of the characteristics of that relationship without pretending to settle the chicken-and-egg controversy. My topical analysis will complement the socio-historical avenues pioneered by Robert Sklar in *Movie-Made America* (1975) and Michael Wood in *America at the Movies* (1975). Some film history is required to fill out the context, and my discussion will reflect the kind of work done by Garth Jowett in *Film: The Democratic Art* (1976) and by Gerald Mast in his mistitled study *A Short History of the Movies* (2nd ed., 1976), the standard references.

Discussion of methodology and history will not be as positive and final as some might like. Much of what I say will be tentative and subjective and, of course, subject to debate. In many ways I hope to stimulate controversy that will assume a dialectical format. However, my analysis of budget and other technical problems will be comprehensive and exact. The process of "producing" a movie-based course is complex and intricate, though it can be readily described. Also, the steps to be followed with the movies are relevant to those with other filmic types and television. Generalizations concerning technical properties are universally applicable.

Finally, because I am a historian whose experience is at the college level, I will rely on circumstances closest to my background and discipline for illustrations and examples. However, this is not a text only for historians or only for college professors. What I have to say is designed for teachers at all levels of instruction. There is an interchangeability of observation that transcends subject matter and audience. That is particularly true in assessing student susceptibility. As an old saying goes, "The only difference between a high school senior and a college freshman is one wild summer." Methods that work in higher education can easily be adapted to high school.

ONE | FILM AS AN EDUCATION MEDIUM

MOTION PICTURES have been an integral part of American life for over three-quarters of a century. Like the bicycle and automobile, they began as playthings of the rich, expensive novelties. But as enterprising businessmen soon discovered that new modes of transportation could be mass-produced profitably, they also realized that a tremendous market existed for a cheap form of popular entertainment. Higher wages and reduced working hours converged to create a circumstance in which truly mass entertainment was possible. More than an industry emerged from the speculative ventures of Adolph Zukor, Cecil B. DeMille, and others. Their products have come to dominate the leisure time of most of the population and have shaped minds in ways that educators have envied.

Until the 1920s, the movies were thought of entirely in terms of entertainment. That motion pictures could also be used to educate people was not even considered until World War I. During the war, George Creel's Committee on Public Information established a Division of Films, which in the last months of the conflict released a few productions. Among those designed to inspire and inform were *Labor's Part in Democracy's War*, *The 1917 Recruit*, and *Woman's Part in the War*. The success of the Creel Committee in marshaling support for the war effort brought praise for its

1

merchandising techniques—some have said that the modern advertising industry grew out of this—and convinced educators that motion pictures could be effectively used in the classroom. One prominent illustration of early instructional films was Yale University's "The Chronicle of America" series, produced in installments during the twenties to complement its book series of the same title. Like so much of American life in the twenties, projectors in the classroom bore witness to the popular belief in the superior quality of machines for improving every facet of human existence.

From those modest beginnings has grown a tradition showing that motion pictures have a place in the classroom. Virtually every teacher has relied on film as a supplement or alternative to his normal oral and literary presentations. That supplementary function has been extended by some who believe that film is the most effective way to communicate with visually responsive students; for them, films have become the primary instructional vehicle.

Though the integration of film into classroom activity has progressed, the evolution has been slow, uneven, and at times uncertain. Pedagogical difficulties, economic considerations, and technological problems have combined to impede systematic and uniform development. But such hazards as volatile nitrate stock (replaced in the late 1940s with nonflammable celluloid) and the high cost of equipment acquisition (mitigated since the mid-1960s by federal funding) have been solved. Modern technology promises to answer those that remain, and the potential of the video disc and the video playback machine are only beginning to be understood. The consulting firm of Arthur D. Little, Inc. predicts that within a decade complete electronic home-entertainment systems will be economically feasible. Movie theaters will become a relic of the past if that transpires, but the market for visual products of all kinds will increase markedly. As Francis Ford Coppola noted at the 1979 Academy Award presentation, we stand on the brink of a tremendous communications revolution.

The kind of motion picture most commonly found in the classroom today is the same as it was fifty years ago. The staple has been the educational film, an instructional production that is frequently called an informational film because of the odious reputation of older educational films. Loosely defined, an educational/informational film is one which educates its viewers about a particular subject or issue that is limited in scope. Didactic considerations take precedence over all others, and every production decision is subordinated to the overall goal of communicating a body of knowledge in the simplest and most direct fashion. For a long time it was assumed that education and entertainment were mutually exclusive functions, and there was no effort to make the viewing of an instructional film a pleasurable experience. Some even believed that it was impossible to merge the two, since one would invariably overwhelm the other.

Encyclopedia Britannica was the pioneer in instructional films. During the 1930s, at a time of economic crisis, its products appealed to school districts in search of inexpensive substitutes. The military, in conjunction with Hollywood luminaries like Frank Capra and Walt Disney, expanded the field during World War II. The force of circumstance—large numbers to be taught a wide variety of subjects by a minimal number of instructors—has been the strongest stimulant for the expansion of educational films. Training films remain an essential ingredient of military life. I once met a veteran who had to undergo six different viewings of *Why Viet Nam?*, a Signal Corps explanation/ justification for the war in Southeast Asia. Industry has also adopted this kind of film as a useful mechanism for indoctrinating new employees and revamping old ones. It is a twentieth-century version of the Lancastrian group-teaching method, taken to its logical extreme. The annual outpouring by the Learning Corporation of America and other producers suggests that the message that films are a cost-efficient way of teaching large numbers has not been lost on educators and administrators either.

A working assumption of the educational film is that it

assists teachers in conveying information that otherwise would be ignored or treated in a cursory, less-than-satisfactory manner. This is the case when a psychologist shows a class a film of an animal in surgery to demonstrate nerve actions. Similarly, educators use films if visual presentation offers the opportunity for communicating information or perspectives in a dramatic or intense fashion. An illustration of this would be an ethics teacher's showing of a motion picture about Hitler's attempt to exterminate the Jews, for example, *Night and Fog*, to augment a literary approach. While such productions may be part of a series, they tend to be episodic in nature. Also, though they may require an entire class period to relay, they continue to be supplementary to more traditional modes of instruction. In today's lexicon they are designed to enrich, not supplant. They are an aid to the instructor and must be tailored to his particular needs.

Because of the didactic dimension of instructional films, there is a tendency to assume that they can substitute for a teacher. The most typical example of this attitude is the instructor who schedules one when he must be absent from class. A more dangerous example is the CBS television series "Sunrise Semester" and its host of imitators. Television in this circumstance is not functioning in accord with the unique properties of the medium but is simply acting as a conduit to convey an instructional film to a larger audience than possible in a classroom or theater. The continuing telecasting of "Sunrise Semester" and the duplication of its approach by others might be used as evidence of its success, but I would vigorously disagree. In the absence of any follow-up to determine what the viewer has learned and the level of understanding he has reached, I question what educational goal has been achieved. A context is necessary for conveying even the most readily understandable material, and it is impossible to do that when relying exclusively on home viewing. College credit is ordinarily available from the sponsoring institution for "Sunrise Semester," but the logistics involved and the difficulty of transferring such credit make it unlikely that many viewers become students. Also, the discipline necessary for careful viewing is lacking in the everyday human situation, except under the most exceptional circumstances. Otherwise, we would have long ago replaced our school system partly or wholly with televised home instruction. It is difficult to say how much unrelated information and useless tidbits of knowledge are gained while shaving or cooking breakfast.

When televised instructional films are given a context through a link with an educational institution, the chances for a valid learning experience are enhanced. Collateral readings, perhaps occasional on-campus instruction, and testing are among the elements which can establish a solid framework. This sort of thing is frequently done on a local level by institutions that own, are affiliated with, or use the services of a public television station. (It is important to realize that public television is not always synonymous with educational television and that the latter term may be a misnomer when applied to any noncommercial telecasting.)

Attempts to go beyond this by utilizing avowedly entertainment programming in the place of instructional films, as was done by many colleges which tried to build courses around the PBS series "The Adams Chronicles" and the ABC series "Roots," have not been markedly successful. The fundamental problem is the same as when a teacher misuses an instructional film: the visual presentation becomes primary, when actually the best it can ever be is supplementary. Motion pictures of every variety, however conveyed, are vehicles assembled to attain predetermined goals. Creating educational aims because they can be arrived at through an available film or program is to reverse the methodological process and constitutes academic prostitution. It is irritating to see the National Education Association "recommend" a television program or film when no explanations are given as to why or to what purpose. Such recommendations only encourage teachers inexperienced in the visual media to misuse film.

The quantity and diversity of instructional films has steadily increased, but quality remains uneven. High production costs can lead to compromises that erode the integrity of the production. Economic factors in this country make it difficult for producers to adhere to the high standards of the British Broadcasting Corporation in its continuing series of literary dramatizations. The BBC places a premium on the precise rendering of place, costume, manner, and feeling. Another continuing difficulty is technological obsolescence. Instructional films are intended to be more lasting than their commercial counterparts, which are designed to capture the public's eye for a relatively short period. Durability is required to justify expenses when tens of thousands if not hundreds of thousands of dollars are involved. A scan of the numerous rental catalogs, many of which are published by colleges and universities seeking to defray purchasing costs, will reveal the great age of many films that remain in circulation. Institutions at all levels, cautious as to what they buy because of limited means, have a habit of keeping instructional films forever. (Whenever possible, administrators prefer outright purchase to rental because they receive something permanent for their expenditure. Short term rentals strike them as a terrible waste of scarce resources.) Because audiences, especially youthful ones, expect the most up-to-date production techniques, they have little patience with older, inferior renderings, and their ability or willingness to learn from them is diminished. Students will laugh at or ignore something that is not on a par with what is offered in the local theater.

The most common failing of educational films can be attributed to the reluctance or inability of producers to fully exploit their potential. Creativity, it would seem, has been left to Hollywood. Typical of this is the infamous "talking face" motion picture, in which all the viewer sees is a filmed lecture no different than the ordinary classroom one. The peculiar visual dimension conceivable in filmed instruction is not tapped even by an occasional cut to a map or other graphic; an audio recording would undoubtedly work just as well. The preponderance of "talking faces" has led to their virtual equation in the mind of students with instructional films and has given that type of motion picture an odious but deserved reputation.

Teachers have ambivalent and sometimes contradictory opinions about instructional pictures and the role they should play. Their eagerness to embrace them is tempered by a concern that they may be replaced by films. Such fears are not without foundation; industry and the military do use films *rather* than instructors. Some colleges and universities even have been turning to educational films and other forms of visual-media instruction principally— perhaps solely—to avoid hiring more teachers. A large midwestern university some years ago made its own "instructional films" by taping the lectures of an economics professor and replaying them when he was on leave. Other institutions have reduced the function of their faculty to answering questions from students who receive their instruction from a composite of viewing films, slides, and television and listening to audio recordings.

Even more unfortunate is the view of teachers who see no redeeming value in filmic instruction and refuse to use them under any circumstance. This media fear is often grounded in a belief that the instructor is the focal point of learning and anything that detracts is subversive. Defining education as a process of human interaction, they view any mechanical aids beyond chalk as detrimental to that process. That attitude, by extension, is also responsible for the widely held conviction that anyone who uses films or other audiovisual materials is an inferior teacher. Film is construed in that view as a crutch instead of an enriching supplement. Because of a chance familiarity with an ill-prepared or absent teacher who throws a film into the breach, these teachers believe that their generalization is proven. A variant of that position is the elitist opinion in many collegiate circles that film is something employed by inferiors either in the education department or in primary and secondary schools.

My evaluation of educational films has been largely negative because I do not like most of them. They are generally of poor quality, devoid of creativity, and conspicuously lacking in conceptualization—all unnecessarily so. Producers of instructional motion pictures have not learned the basic lesson that their competitors in Hollywood, both the movie colony and Television City, recognized from the onset: one can educate and entertain at the same time. (When I use the word entertain, I am doing so in the strict literal sense of holding the attention of the audience.) Those are neither contradictory nor mutually exclusive goals in one presentation. How Hollywood has so successfully educated while entertaining will be discussed in more detail later, but it is imperative to realize that learning is more palatable when coated with some entertainment. I am not suggesting that education become a dog or pony show, but I do think, to twist Neil Postma's observation, that teaching can be a subversive activity. The road to wisdom does not have to be as formidable as the road to Oz. Every instructor knows that he must be in part a performer, that his "act" must be enlivening while enlightening. I ask no more of instructional films.

The entertainment dimension is especially important when television is the medium of instruction. Today's generation sees television almost exclusively as an entertainment vehicle; and if the classroom employs television as an instructional vehicle, they will expect the presentation to be just as enjoyable as their evening diversions. But it is of greater importance for teachers to understand that television viewing does not command the students' attention the way a projected motion picture will. Though I will discuss this circumstance in more detail later, suffice it to say that the size of the television receiver mitigates against its successful use. If it is necessary to use television to convey an instructional film, I highly recommend the use of the newer movie-like, large-screen receivers. The size of the image alone will rivet students' attention as a standard machine will not.

Second in age to the educational film, but better thought of pedagogically, is the documentary. The documentary tradition parallels—though at a slower growth rate—that of instructional productions. It was developed by Robert Flaherty in the 1920s, and his pioneer effort, *Nanook of the North* (1922), was so commercially popular that he was invited to Hollywood. However, his work there was considered unsatisfactory, since the studio believed that its entertainment value was insufficient. His study of idyllic life on a South Sea island, *Moana* (1926), was equal to that of his exploration of Eskimo life, but Hollywood expected native dancing girls. The novelty of *Nanook* had faded, and audiences did not find *Moana* sufficiently entertaining. Flaherty left America for the more congenial environment of England, where the work of John Grierson, Paul Rotha, and others received the sponsorship of the British government and greater public acceptance. There his reputation grew with such productions as *Man of Iran* (1934) and *Elephant Boy* (1937).

Flaherty's preliminary work was expanded in the thirties by Pare Lorenz, but he too found that documentaries were too great a financial risk without government assistance. Lorenz's best-known works, *The Plow That Broke the Plains* (1936) and *The River* (1937), were produced by the Department of Agriculture. In 1937 he convinced the government to establish the United States Film Service, but it was short-lived because of the congressional opposition which viewed it as a propaganda arm of the New Deal.

Like instructional films, documentary productions were greatly stimulated by government needs during World War II. Reflecting on the accomplishments of the German propagandist Leni Riefenstahl in *Triumph of Will* (1934) and *The Olympiad* (1936), the government turned to Hollywood for assistance in promoting the war effort. From this stimulus came *The Memphis Belle* (1942), *The Village of San Pietro* (1944), and others by such respected directors as John Ford and John Huston.

The wartime stimulus was reinforced by the new

medium of television. Network news departments found the documentary to be analogous to their ordinary work and a convenient means of meeting FCC requirements for public service. Entertainment divisions liked them because they made a handy filler when sports programs and feature movies did not end on the hour. Hollywood was also influenced after World War II by Italian neo-realism and its lifelike presentations, and a large number of movies from Henry Hathaway's *The House on 92nd Street* (1945) to Elia Kazan's *On the Waterfront* (1954) came to resemble documentaries.

The documentary has had a sustained life on television, and the films are generally released rather quickly for classroom usage. Many students do not even realize that such presentations as the CBS "Biography" series or the innumerable David L. Wolper productions were first on television. Ratings for televised documentaries have traditionally been poor when compared with strictly entertainment programming; yet many advertisers such as IBM Corporation and Xerox Corporation are willing to sponsor them—not without sound advertising reasoning. Viewer research has revealed that documentary audiences are usually skewed by a disproportionately large number of highly educated decision makers, the kind of people instrumental in the purchase of computers and photocopying machines.

The word "documentary" is commonly used to identify two, perhaps as many as four, distinct filmic types. Strictly speaking, a documentary is what a historian would term a "primary source." It is an attempt by a filmmaker to visually document a subject, the kind of thing that Robert Flaherty attempted when he recorded the lifestyles of Eskimos, South Sea islanders, and Irish fishermen. The effort is to film in an immediate, thorough, and factual manner, with the flow of events dictating form and content. The filmmaker acts as a witness or reporter, with no script involved; the camera documents real activity as it transpires, with a premium on objectivity. This last factor—objectivity—is the most important, for audiences are expected to believe that what they are seeing is absolutely truthful. Integrally united with objectivity are accuracy and authenticity as among the objectives for which the documentarian strives. These qualities are essential because of the filmmaker's desire to educate and inform. Lorenz, for example, did not always abide by the canons of objectivity, thus raising the anger of political critics; one could argue that he was not a documentarian in the classical tradition. The City (1939) is the best illustration of Lorenz as a polemicist rather than a documentarian.

"Documentary" is also used to describe what in fact is a compilation film. So often is the term used this way that most people today, unfamiliar with true form, equate the two. A compilation film is what a historian would call a secondary source, the opinion of a later compiler as opposed to an eyewitness account. Initially, this may be hard to understand because what is seen is real; it is actual footage of something that happened. The filmed material, normally a primary source, becomes secondary by virtue of how it is used by the producer/director.

With a compilation product, the filmmaker either takes his camera with script in hand to shoot predetermined scenes, or he may ignore the camera entirely and comb film archives for his footage. The film is selected from its disparate sources and assembled and edited according to plan, and a narration is added to provide continuity. An illustration of this type of approach is the recently syndicated television series "America Between the Wars," or virtually any of the dozens of war histories from "Victory at Sea" to "The World at War." The objectivity of the classic documentary is replaced by a subjectivity through which a compilation film can easily digress into propaganda. The producer-director assembles a compilation film because he wants to convey a message, and everything is done to facilitate that. The narration is paramount because it is the vehicle used to bring home what could be missed or misunderstood in viewing. The award-winning "documentary" Hyde Park falls into this category. Though filmed entirely on location, it was done according to plan by the

Hyde Park, New York Visual Environment Committee to call attention to visual pollution in its community and the nation at large.

An interesting experiment is to take a compilation production and dub in a sound track contradictory to the original. One will be surprised to discover how readily audiences respond to the new "interpretation." (Try this particularly with any episode of the 1950s "Biography" television series, narrated by Mike Wallace in his inimitable style from scripts scathing in their criticism or fulsome in their praise.)

Occasionally, films that purport to be documentaries in the classical sense are in fact compilations, and it is virtually impossible to visually separate the two. When Louis De Rochemont reenacted scenes for his *March of Time* series, viewers did not know the difference between the reenactment and the real thing any more than they did in 1898 when Vitagraph claimed that *Tearing Down the Spanish Flag* was filmed in the heat of battle instead of on a Manhattan rooftop. The old newsreels did this regularly; when cameras came late to the scene, they simply had it repeated if possible.

The third kind of film usually falling under the term "documentary" is not a documentary at all but is an information or instructional film. People think these are documentaries because they frequently incorporate stock footage of bygone events and because they are produced by the same individuals the public associates with documentaries, often network news departments. The kind of productions I have in mind are the widely known CBS presentations "Hunger in America," "K.K.K.: The Invisible Empire," and "The Selling of the Pentagon." NBC's "White Paper" and "Project Twenty" series are other illustrations. Usually they are nothing more than in-depth reporting, sometimes with historical perspective provided by library stock. They are sold to the public, later appearing in school media libraries, as objective documentaries—at least until someone complains. Such was the case with "The Selling of the Pentagon," a production that drew such criticism that CBS telecast a rebuttal.

The degree to which these information-cum-documentaries are believed and influence people's opinions and actions is borne out in the response to Edward R. Murrow's 1954 assault on Joseph McCarthy. His documentary-like presentation, culled from film in CBS's files, appeared on "See It Now." It is credited by historians with swaying public opinion against McCarthy, signaling his end.

Television has further muddied the waters for appreciating what is and what is not a documentary by its creation of "docu-dramas." Traditionally, in Hollywood and on television, these have been simply costume dramas. Studio publicity departments often made claims for accuracy and authenticity in their renditions, and their extravagance has, of course, been exceeded by television. "Docu-dramas" are no more than recreations. They lack the immediacy of the true documentary and the actuality of the compilation. They do, however, provide the illusion of reality. But who knows about the productions' factual integrity or objectivity of interpretation? It would be best to dismiss the term, as was done when the writer Truman Capote tried to sell *In Cold Blood* as nonfiction fiction. However, that is not likely to happen. As the "new journalism" permits the reporter to blend the real with imitation and even fiction, "docu-dramas" will probably continue to be sold as essentially truthful.*

I find this development frightening because docu-dramas such as "Roots" and "Holocaust" are proving to be enormously popular and critically acclaimed. The televised adaptation of "Backstairs at the White House" and James Michner's "Centennial" are likely to repeat those successes, among other things superseding John Ford-John Wayne westerns for today's generation and its understanding of how the West was "won." Furthermore, while

---

*The phrases "literature of fact" and "documentary fiction," as well as "faction," have recently appeared to describe the literary intermeshing of fact and fiction and to legitimate that intermeshing. (See "In Defense of the Television 'Docu-Drama' " by David W. Rintels, *New York Times*, April 22, 1979.)

opinion is not unanimous, scholars have defended them as "essentially accurate," even if some of the detail is erroneous or exaggerated. One academic, an advisor for a docudrama which was merchandised to schools as an educational film, described for me his standard. If something happened, regardless of place or context, or if it could have happened, then it was perfectly acceptable to film the scene and sell it as both authentic and representative. Producer-director Dore Schary informed me that that had been his attitude too when he was involved in such "biopics" as *Edison the Man* (1940), described by one reviewer as "facts and MGM fantasy combine[d] well in a sentimental treatment." What was important, Schary believed, was to capture the "essence" of the man and not to worry about details. But when he began to shoot a picture about a man he knew and admired, Franklin D. Roosevelt in *Sunrise at Campobello* (1960), he came to realize that the essence was not enough. Adherence to the facts, large and small, was essential. His conversion should be an instructive example for docu-dramatists.

Documentaries—classical, compilation, informational, and docu-dramatic—are extremely popular among teachers. Social scientists, particularly historians and political scientists, are avid fans with a preference for the compilation variety. They see in them an opportunity for resurrecting past episodes that students did not experience. The immediacy, the sense of reality, and the presumed accuracy and objectivity captivate students and instructors alike. Previously "dead" subject matter suddenly comes alive. The rationale is this: why just talk and read about the 1920s when you can see them in *The Golden Twenties* or *The Jazz Age?* The appeal to students is unmistakable when one can show them *The Rise and Fall of Nazi Germany* in seventeen minutes instead of asking them to read more than a thousand pages of *The Rise and Fall of the Third Reich.*

Unlike instructional films, documentaries have achieved such a high level of acceptance that few are inclined to criticize their use in the classroom—so long as they do not appear too frequently. Overuse, a subjective evaluation, will lead to a negative reaction by colleagues and administrators. That will occur because the legitimacy of documentaries is grounded in their supplementary function. They are considered valid for enrichment because of their realistic, lifelike, and recreative qualities. Too frequent appearances may be interpreted as a sign of laziness by the instructor or, worse still, indicative that he or she is using them as substitutes. But ordinarily, few envision documentaries as threatening substitutes because of their obvious inability to survive without a context provided by lectures and readings.

Critics are likely to raise two objections about documentaries. The first is the obvious one that subject matter is limited to events after the invention of the motion picture camera in the 1890s. This is not so much a criticism as it is a recognition of a limitation. If one accepts the validity of docu-dramas, or if one agrees with art critic Harold Rosenberg that filmed versions of literary classics are "valid substitutes" for a nonreading public, then even that limitation can be transcended.

The second criticism should be as plain as the first, but too often it goes unrecognized. I believe that the dual problems of objectivity and accuracy should receive greater attention from teachers. The classical documentary is by definition objective and accurate, and as an immediate record of reality it could not be anything else. Such a firm guarantee does not accompany the more popular compilation work, yet the tendency has been to assume such is true. The American public has been led to believe that all of those things called documentaries are true simply because they appear realistic and are not obviously staged. It makes no difference if the viewing is in the classroom or the living room; we have been conditioned to accept them uncritically. The verisimilitude, the very reason instructors show documentaries, sears into the viewer's consciousness an image not soon to be forgotten.

That the public so gullibly accepts all documentaries

as truthful and accurate is understandable when one considers how much time and effort have gone into popularizing such a myth. Even standard dictionary definitions further reinforce that misconception. For example, the lexicographers for *The American Heritage Dictionary of the English Language* define documentary as "presenting facts objectively without editorializing or inserting fictional material" and "a television or motion-picture presentation of factual, political, social, or historical events or circumstances, often consisting of actual news films accompanied by narration." Unfortunately, film scholars such as John Harrington *(The Rhetoric of Film)*, who routinely append glossaries to their studies, have not found the misconception serious enough to warrant the inclusion of a definition of "documentary" that is in keeping with its heritage. Harrington and others instead rely on vague textual descriptions such as that offered by John Grierson, who coined the term. Grierson defined documentary as "the creative treatment of actuality," a definition that is attractive but incomplete. Historian David Culbert recently attempted a comprehensive, albeit cumbersome definition. Documentary is "all methods of recording on celluloid any aspect of reality interpreted whether by factual shooting or by sincere and justifiable reconstruction, so as to appeal either to reason or emotion, for the purpose of stimulating the desire for, and the widening of human knowledge and understanding, and of truthfully posing problems and their solutions in the spheres of economics, culture, and human relations."

My concern with objectivity in documentaries, particularly the compilation variety, is not universally shared. Tim Hewat, a BBC producer, argues that a documentarian "goes into some subjects with a prejudice or belief that he wants to see borne out on the screen...." His opinion is that "it is the responsibility of the producer to draw conclusions from the information" and make his position on the issue clear. Similarly, Robert Sklar has criticized "The New Klan," a 1978 production developed for the Corporation for Public Broadcasting, for not offering a perspective on the facts. Rather than praise the producers for their attempts at objectivity, he assails their presumption that "facts alone could make up for a point of view." Sklar would presumably be more satisfied with something like the 1976 Academy Award-winning documentary *Harlan County, U.S.A.*, a film that unmistakably promotes a point of view—the miner's position in their contract struggle with management. I might be more sympathetic to the attitudes of Hewat and Sklar if viewers were less naive and more aware of the subjective nature of those films so loosely and casually called documentaries. I surely cannot agree with Hewat's contention that some sort of balance or objectivity can be achieved by encouraging producers with differing prejudices.

Teachers have an obligation when screening a documentary to inform the students that what they will see, especially in compilations, is an interpretation, that the picture was edited and assembled by someone trying to put across a message. Instead of always selecting materials in harmony with our viewpoints, we should occasionally project something directly contradictory. That might drive home to students the point that they need a factual standard of reference for evaluating documentaries and that they must apply their own critical viewing skills. New viewing habits developed by teachers might continue and students might be willing to intellectually challenge the steady stream of televised documentaries. Rather than accept them as the final word on the subject, students might be inclined to pursue the subject in more detail.

Unlike most instructional productions, I do find the typical documentary visually satisfying. Its popularity is understandable. My criticisms are directed at its use. What is required is a more sophisticated methodology than what is normally in use. An informational film, while it can never serve as a valid teacher substitute, can fairly well survive on its own merits within limited circumstances. One can reach a circumscribed pedagogical goal by showing one, though anything more involved than the "care and cleaning of the M-1 rifle" calls for additional support. A documentary, on the other hand, will be a meaningless exercise without a context; something must go before it and something must follow it. Collateral experiences, readings, lectures, and so forth are necessary. To date, most teachers have used them only to prove the actuality of what they have described or to verify the accuracy of their descriptions. But that kind of supplementary activity is too limited, myopic, and one-dimensional. I have suggested other ways in which they might be shown, such as challenging students with selected screenings of those with which we disagree. Later I will recommend additional methodological approaches.

The filmic form that has entered the academic scene most recently is the commercial Hollywood feature picture. There is a definite but understandable irony that the oldest film genre would be the last to find its way into the educational world. The introduction of the movies into the classroom accompanied what Thomas Brandon has termed the "film explosion" that followed World War II. That explosion reflected the recognition of the movies—at least those of foreign origin—as an art form worthy of study, something the poet Vachel Lindsay had urged in 1915 in *The Art of the Motion Picture*. Gilbert Seldes had also included the movies in his survey of *The Seven Lively Arts* in 1924.

Brandon and his distributing company, Brandon Films, forerunner of today's Macmillian-Audio-Brandon Films, were largely responsible for introducing American audiences to international cinema. The presumption, as is so often the case in our cultural observations, was that Europe was light years ahead of Americans in the art of cinema. Whereas Hollywood understood only the entertainment dimension of the movies, European directors supposedly appreciated the full range of the communicative force. They purportedly transformed it into a vehicle for studied self-expression analogous to the novel and other printed arts. The French periodical *Cahiers du Cinema* began speaking of directors as *auteurs*, authors of a motion picture in a manner similar—for comparable reasons and with the same degree of independence—to their literary counterparts.

An occasional American such as Orson Welles, with his *Citizen Kane* (1941), might be included in this select group, but the propensity was to dismiss American directors and their productions as unworthy of examination and analysis. Hollywood, the studio system, and the premium on profits reinforced the belief that the domestic cinema was a business, not an art form. Eventually that attitude would change when independent producer-directors like Stanley Kramer began to replace the decaying studios as the mainstay of the industry. Critics would start discussing American cinema within the same artistic framework, and the film critic would rapidly assume a position of prominence and public recognition far beyond that of his peers working with other popular arts. The very word "cinema" became important, for it was and continues to be used to differentiate those movies with aesthetic merit from the commonplace entertainment variety.

As art movie houses sprang up around the country to take advantage of the new awareness of the movies, colleges and a few high schools also began to incorporate film study into their curriculum. Unlike documentaries and educational films, however, the movies were studied for themselves rather than engaged as instructional aids. The most common format was a film appreciation course, though film history was sometimes included. A few institutions, notably the University of California at Los Angeles, also initiated courses in the art and technique of motion picture production. Film appreciation was normally found in the art or fine arts department, and screening focused on Jean Renoir, Ingmar Bergman, Vittorio De Sica, and other European *auteurs*.

As a stepchild in the art department, film appreciation soon stagnated. No consideration was given to how movies might be used in other instructional capacities. Except in a very limited fashion, most educators, like most of the public, were unable to transcend the perception that the movies were purely entertainment; and entertainment had no place in the classroom. The humorist Russell Baker has summarized that belief: "Even at their best, movies can probably be nothing more than entertainment for the child imprisoned in the oldest of us." Teachers, film critic Vincent Canby has noted, were part of a larger community "brought up knowing that movies were a lesser form of literature. . . ."

The exile of the movies in the art department eventually ended. A change took place, documented and encouraged by the National Council of Teachers of English in *Motion Pictures and the Study of English* (1965). Specialists in literature had been interested in all forms of popular culture since the 1930s, principally as a branch of literary criticism. Convinced that they could not ignore the subject, they embraced the distinction between serious and popular culture and tried to quarantine the latter. (For a reflection of this mentality, see the frequently reprinted essay "Masscult and Midcult" by Dwight Macdonald.) Others applied the canons of serious criticism to popular culture only to discover that many of the elements of high culture could be found in the mass media. It is this latter group that was responsible for calling attention to the movies in the 1960s.

The attempt of the N.C.T.E. to bring the movies under its umbrella was shortsighted, and its viewpoint was selfish and exploitative. The movies were significant for this group because of the way they "illuminate and augment the study of literature." After languishing in obscurity, George Bluestone's *Novels into Film* (1957) was quickly reissued in paperback to meet the demand. Competition between English and fine arts departments flared as "The Rhetoric of Film" was pitted against "Film Appreciation," each seeking to entice the other's students. But little discernible difference existed between the two, with the possible exception that more Hollywood pictures showed up in the rhetoric classes. Yet what the N.C.T.E. was advocating represented a significant departure: movies were being sanctified as instructional assistants comparable to documentaries and educational films.

The movement promoted by the N.C.T.E. has grown

furthest not in traditional English departments but in American Studies curricula and those places where popular culture has achieved a modicum of respectability. Dispensing with the artificial constraints imposed by a high culture/low culture dichotomy, scholars like Peter Rollins and Carol Obertubbesing have shown what can be accomplished with a little intellectual imagination. (See "American Studies and Film: A Crisis for the Humanities and a Model Course," distributed by the National Humanities Institute, New Haven, Conn.) In their hands, the movies are viewed as a mirror of American society and thus become a means for examining our culture "through the looking glass." They still dissect movies as one would in film appreciation, but their intent is not to uncover artistic conventions. Instead, they illustrate how the movies have interacted with the cultural ethos. American Studies and popular culture teachers have gone far beyond the modest suggestions of the N.C.T.E. and are coming dangerously close to slipping the confines of their parent discipline. Hybrid as they are, it is sometimes difficult to distinguish them from social historians.

Heartened by the success of their competitors, success defined and measured by the number of students in a classroom, historians "discovered" the movies. Political scientists, sociologists, and others in the liberal arts were not far behind, and instructors in secondary schools soon became similarly intrigued with the possibilities of showing movies. Few complete courses were built around the movies, since the tendency was to integrate them into traditional offerings the same way documentaries were. Whether this trend would have developed without the enrollment crisis of the seventies is debatable. My own feeling is that it would not have. But faced as they were with shrinking classes, those in the liberal arts were willing to resort to any technique to revive their flagging popularity.

Unfortunately, here was a case in which a subject area was opened and an instructional methodology was attempted before the preliminary research had been carried out. The normal course of academic events is the reverse: research opens new vistas and new approaches, which are in turn incorporated into the curriculum. Consequently, methodological problems have been and still are rampant. Had academic interest in the movies followed the same path as it did in econometrics, occurring at roughly the same time, many of the pitfalls could have been avoided. Research into econometrics as both a pedagogical resource and as a subdiscipline smoothed its transition into the classroom.

Thus far, historians have been the most aggressive professionals in the liberal arts for bringing the movies into the classroom. Ten years ago no history department sponsored a movie-oriented course. Today over thirty departments, with several thousand students annually, offer movie-oriented courses, and virtually every department has offerings in which the movies are a supplementary aspect. The process of legitimation has followed the usual procedures, including the formation of the Historians' Film Committee, an affiliate of the American Historical Association. The committee publishes *Film and History*, a compendium that mixes articles examining some aspects of film history with exchanges on the latest instructional methodologies. Interest by historians in film has quickly spread abroad, and in 1975 scholars from five nations formed the International Association for Audio-Visual Media in Historical Research and Education. The American Historical Association was so taken by the idea of introducing movies into the curriculum that it directed a project for editing features such as *Juarez* (1939) and *Luther* (1957) to fit a standard class period. The project has been discontinued because of costs and disputes over the validity of the process, but the commercial distributor Films Incorporated has tried to resurrect the concept by editing *The Grapes of Wrath* (1940) and several other well-known productions.

The deluge of feature movies into higher education and secondary schools has caused considerable confusion and controversy. Much of the criticism stems from ignorance about the purposes and goals of those who show the movies. The long-held prejudice that American movies are solely an entertainment medium has proved to be a formidable barrier to reasoned dialogue. Since it is usually the younger and untenured teachers who have been quickest to turn to the movies, departmental generation gaps are deepened. The reservoir of hostility and suspicion against all forms of audiovisual instruction is most easily focused on the least understood. Fear of the unknown and jealousy over the success in attracting students are two more factors that help explain why the situation is more of an argument than a debate. The number of film sessions at professional meetings and an occasional grant or degree do not confer legitimacy or acceptability. If anything, a careful examination of the subject matter of the sessions or the grant proposals will reveal that they are oriented toward research, not pedagogy. Discussion of innovative teaching techniques lacks the glamor and prestige of research ventures. This pathology demands that more missionary work be done before the movies are in fact embraced as appropriate and proper for classroom use.

MOVIES IN THE CLASSROOM: WHY?

Much of the controversy could be avoided if the advocates of movie-based instruction spent some time explaining why they are showing movies. These instructors have been their own worst enemies by failing to address this fundamental question. There have been conversations concerning the how of things, methodology, but even those discussions usually take place among those who are already engaged.

The reason for this omission may be self-evident in that many have not seriously thought through why they do it, beyond the simple observation that screening movies fills classrooms. Administrators like to hear that kind of explanation. Large enrollments justify substantial budgets, and the logic is readily grasped. So important has the enrollment problem been in the liberal arts and so easy has it been for movie courses to diminish it that many have not thought it necessary to go any further with their explanations. And they may not have a better justification than the observation of film educator John M. Culkin: "Today's students have a special thing going with the movies. They turn on when the projector gets turned on." (See his article "Films Deliver" in J. M. Culkin and Anthony Schillaci, eds., *Films Deliver* [1970].)

But those who have stopped short are beginning to be severely criticized by others who have more valid reasons for why they are showing movies. The most outspoken has been Stuart Samuels, the historian whose pungent analysis "Film in the History Curriculum: Numbing or Nourishing?" contends that film study in history often is "a lot of bullshit" with "little careful attention." Although I might not express myself in such earthy phrases, I agree. Further, I do not believe that the situation is limited to history courses on the college level. One large Long Island high school holds weekly screenings, ostensibly as part of its language arts program, but in reality as a study hall alternative. The "course" has no structure, and it continues because it keeps students in school and out of trouble.

I do not wish to be too critical of the propositions that movie-based classes are good for enrollments or that they are responsible for reducing truancy. Those are valid justifications which address real concerns. They are comparable to the practical arguments heard after World War I that physical education was necessary in the schools because medical examinations during the war brought out the poor condition of draftees. But practical explanations are incomplete. The primary function of the schools is to educate minds, and an intellectual defense must be provided for any innovation. Physical education never developed an intellectual rationale, and to this day it is regularly scorned by many as a "frill" that does not belong. Movie-based instruction will have the same experience if teachers do not develop justifications beyond the practical.

The most prevalent intellectual reason given for bringing movies into the classroom is that they visualize and dramatize subject matter. John O'Connor speaks for many when he observes that "movies bring historical characters to life and help to re-create the atmosphere of another time . . . [they] offer a heightened sense of the 'feel' of an era. . . ." From that perspective, movies are analogous in their use to documentaries: they have an illustrative function. Numerous examples are available. The historian who wants his students to better appreciate the plight of the downtrodden during the Great Depression will turn to William Wellman's *Wild Boys of the Road* (1933) or John Ford's *The Grapes of Wrath* (1940). Movies like Robert Rossen's *All the King's Men* (1949) or John Ford's *The Last Hurrah* (1958) can be vehicles through which a political scientist exposes the inner workings of the political boss system. Similarly, a psychologist might screen Nunnally Johnson's *The Three Faces of Eve* (1957) to help his or her students grasp schizophrenia. *The Snake Pit* (1948) provides sociologists and psychologists with a strong illustration of mental illness and how public asylums treat it. Constructing an entire course in this way is difficult, but occasional usage à la documentaries is frequently done. The fact that all of these examples are screen versions of successful novels is no accident either. Engaging a piece of fiction to dramatize a concept has been an academic staple for decades, and a filmic presentation of the same can draw sustenance from that precedent.

However, the illustrative explanation for the use of film is unfortunately very limited in its application. Few productions are likely to meet instructional standards for accuracy, authenticity, and thoroughness. They are also in every instance an interpretation by someone else, and the teacher may agree or disagree as he does with documentaries. Film critic Vincent Canby's statement about *Grease* (1978) could not be more accurate: "It is not a recreation of the 1950's; it is what someone thought the 1950's were like." Those that meet the standards appear time and time again, until they become, in the words of one distributor's brochure, "Classics for the Classroom."

While I have shown movies for illustrative purposes, I have become reluctant to present that as the reason why I organize courses around feature pictures. I am hesitant to sponsor a movie on the grounds that it is a reliably historical rendition of the subject because I do not want to vouch for the totality of its information and interpretation. Like Dore Schary, I am no longer satisfied that capturing the essence of the subject is sufficient. Every movie contains too many errors or omissions of fact for my historical standards, and it is too cumbersome and uncertain to try to correct them. Students are disposed to believe everything they see, as they do everything they read. There is no guarantee that a teacher's verbal correction will expunge misimpressions ingrained in their consciousness by dramatic and compelling presentations. I am not arguing that it cannot be done—only that it is a difficult task.

If one does select a movie for illustrative purposes, I strongly urge that one not show it in the same course that also includes documentaries. Some may organize classes around a mixture of feature films and documentaries—in fact, many do—but I oppose that integration. Each form calls for separate viewing skills, differing degrees of visual literacy, and varying assumptions about authenticity and validity. Students have been conditioned to believe documentaries unhesitatingly, and mixing the two forms will encourage them to transfer that unquestioning attitude to movies as well. They are inclined to do that anyway, and I do not believe teachers should promote that tendency. As I said earlier, I believe that instructors should be teaching and insisting upon critical viewing with all filmic forms.

The hazards inherent in the illustrative approach to teaching with the movies are intensified when the scene shifts from the strict confines of the classroom to less controlled educational settings such as museums and libraries. The popularity of movie-based instruction in the schools has encouraged these institutions to expand beyond their travelogues and nostalgia-induced series into other areas, such as history. The American Library Association has been recommending film acquisitions for libraries for over a quarter of a century, though none have been feature films. Recently, funding from the National Endowment for the Humanities and comparable state agencies has provided the means for long-term leases of commercial productions. Consequently, nearly every library or museum in America now sponsors regular screenings as part of its public service.

Usually there is no particular format, but the bicentennial celebration stimulated many to invite the public to a chronicle of the American heritage via Hollywood scenarios. The normal course was to screen the movies with little or no cautionary introduction, or any discussion about accuracy. The result was that the prestige and authority of the institution was transferred to the movie, and viewers went home thinking they had witnessed an authentic historical rendition. Worse yet, many PBS outlets sponsored "film festivals" of United States history, exposing even larger audiences to Hollywood "history" without considering how they might be misleading their viewers. Because of the high opinion that most people have for PBS and their concurrent assumption that "educational" television is just that, their natural inclination to believe Hollywood was deepened.

If the intellectual environment surrounding public teaching situations can be enhanced, the illustrative technique can be as successful there as in the classroom. A museum in a medium-sized Midwestern city is trying to do that in a year-long series of thirty-one movies about America's past. In addition to the screenings, there are discussions about how motion pictures captured or distorted certain events or incidents. The discussion leader is a local newspaper film critic who tries to engage a specialist each week to help sort out fact from fiction. However, these discussions are optional, and expert commentary cannot be guaranteed. While I think that this venture is far superior to most of its competition, I remain dubious that viewers will be enlightened rather than confirmed in their misimpressions. Film critics are not historians. And those viewers who do not remain for the discussion after the showing will be intellectually poorer for having uncritically taken in a film under the auspices of an educational institution.

The preferred reason for bringing movies into the classroom is more involved than the basic illustrative approach. At the risk of using confusing terminology, I call it the "documentarian" function because the method is to examine, analyze, and evaluate movies just as any documents would do. The method virtually ignores aesthetic qualities while focusing attention on how the film/document treats the subject in question.

This approach will naturally raise the question "why"; my answer is grounded in several assumptions. The first is that much if not most of what students and the general public learn is gained from movies, television, and similar visual-media productions. This could once be said of works of fiction, but they have been reduced in importance in what is sometimes called our "post-literate" society. One may or may not accept that assumption, but our disagreement would probably be one of degree rather than of kind. John Harrington has calculated that the average college freshman has accumulated a stockpile of 17,000 hours of viewing time. Industry research has revealed that the typical movie audience is composed of people 17-30 years old with higher than average formal education. On the basis of such facts and other subjective evidence, I am willing to assert that the educational system is clearly second to movies and television as the primary source of information for most Americans. In a similar vein, surveys have consistently revealed that most people rely on televised news for their awareness of the day's events; the steady demise of daily newspapers confirms that. Popular confirmation of my thesis was recently addressed by *Newsweek* in its May 7, 1979 cover story "TV Comedy: What It's Teaching the Kids." I am delighted that even in this limited excursion the general public is beginning to be acquainted with the fact that movie and television watching does constitute a learning experience.

The second assumption is that, because the normal viewer lacks a factual standard of reference with which to compare and evaluate what he sees, he will be inclined to believe everything before him. Only in those circumstances in which the viewer knows something about the subject or thinks—accurately or inaccurately—that he does, will he even dispute a screen rendition. (That kind of dispute does not happen often, but when it does, the derision can be intense. For example, when John Wayne's rendition of the war in Vietnam, *The Green Berets* [1968], was shown to American combat soldiers, roars of laughter drowned out the dialogue.) Add to the credulity of audiences the verisimilitude of visual production, the efforts of directors to enhance a movie's credibility, and the attempts of publicists to sway opinion before viewing. The "preconditioning" for *Grease* is the latest illustration of the growing prominence of advertising budgets. The audience is almost certain to be victimized. Matters become more critical in view of the fact that critical viewing skills are virtually nonexistent and that the state of visual literacy is every bit as bad as the well-documented condition of print literacy. Just because everyone can see does not mean that everyone views with an eye for evaluating and judging.

A third assumption is that one cannot distinguish between the entertainment and educational dimensions of the movies. To do so is artificial and to deny that both functions take place simultaneously. I am not saying that people attend feature films with the preconceived idea that they will learn something. They may feel that way with documentaries and educational films, but not with movies. People go to theaters or turn on a movie on television to be entertained; yet they do not realize that their mind is being saturated with information of greater or lesser importance the whole time. As in the case of reading, the public expects to have its beliefs reaffirmed, and whether a movie is "liked" in large measure depends on that reaffirmation. Because the movie industry is a profit-making business, most producers want their directors to convey messages with which viewers agree. Those who do not, such as

Stanley Kramer, who tried to change attitudes about race relations in *The Defiant Ones* (1958) and questioned victor's justice in *Judgment at Nuremberg* (1961), suffer at the box office.

The desire to reaffirm is only in effect, however, when Hollywood has reason to assume that audiences know something about the subject. Most of the time audiences do not know or have forgotten, perhaps preferring a nostalgic rendition to a re-creation of reality. An instance of the former is organized crime: most people think that they know a lot about it, whereas in fact they do not. Consequently, Francis Ford Coppola's *Godfather I* and *II* (1972 and 1974) become their text. As for the latter, the war in Vietnam has been over for less than five years, and yet I will venture that the spate of films about it in 1978, Hal Ashby's *Coming Home*, Sidney J. Furie's *The Boys in Company C*, Jeremy Paul Kagan's *Heroes*, and Michael Cimino's *The Deerhunter*, for example, will have a more lasting impression than all of the newspaper or television reports. For the 17-25-year-old group, Vietnam is little-known history too, and it will rely on the movies for information about it just as it will turn to *Animal House* (1978) for an understanding of college life during the same period.

I do not contend that students and the public at large always learn great and significant things in their viewing. Sometimes they do, as when an entire generation was educated about the Civil War by Victor Fleming's *Gone With the Wind* (1939), or when hundreds of John Ford, Howard Hawks, and Raoul Walsh westerns were the sourcebooks for understanding Indians. Usually the process of learning is repetitive and accumulative, with small bits of information and interpretation, often trivial in nature, piling one on top of the other. A vast storehouse of "knowledge" grows up, in which truth and fiction are melded.

It is readily accepted that Hollywood has been the instructional mainstay for foreigners' perceptions about America. The reverse is also usually held to be true. I am suggesting that we go a step further and realize that people unconsciously or unwittingly rely on the movies for general information and understanding of many things. Lawyers in several current cases are trying to prove that movies and their televised counterparts are capable of influencing human behavior to the degree that viewers duplicate crimes they see on the screen. If that is possible, if movies are that strong a motivating force in individual circumstances, then it is not hard to believe that they are a significant learning force as well.

Working from my assumptions, I have brought movies into the classroom. My discipline is history, but the approach is equally valid for all disciplines in the humanities. The first step is to sharpen the students' viewing skills, to improve their visual literacy. That step has to be repeated with each class. With that foundation, the teacher must then provide them with a factual standard of reference. The reference point includes not only information about the subject matter of the film but material relevant to the social milieu in which it appeared. The assumption here is that movies are not produced in a vacuum. Doing this takes two weeks of the course, during which not a single movie is screened. When the first feature does appear, it is treated as a document that must be compared and contrasted with the best sources available.

If the public were not so gullible, if our country were not, as Robert Sklar has so aptly described it, "movie-made," the "documentarian" reason for bringing movies into the classroom might be unnecessary. There would have to be another raison d'etre. But that is not the circumstance. Movies, every bit as much as documentaries and instructional films, have been educative forces in our society, and we must learn to deal with them on their own terms.

TWO | THE MOVIES: MIRROR ON THE WALL OR WINDOW TO THE WORLD?

THE HISTORIC interrelationship between the movies and American society is something that academics have only recently begun to probe intensely. Recognition of the importance of the subject was slow in emerging because of intellectual prejudices and misconceptions about the movies themselves. Hollywood's dream factory produced opiates for the masses, and presumably what was of interest to the masses was thought to be of no concern for serious researchers. Those attitudes have experienced a substantial change in the last decade, and there is a heightened awareness today that the icons of popular culture are among the best clues for understanding social development. The word "society" has also been redefined and extended to include the masses as well as the educated, articulate elite.

As an awareness of the significant interaction between the movies and society has evolved, scholars have come to realize that the relationship is complex and does not lend itself to easy analysis. The perspectives and skills necessary for unraveling its intricacies have had to be formulated and they have yet to mature fully. A distinct tendency to observe and comment on what is self-evident remains commonplace. Indicative of that continuing inclination toward the obvious is the often repeated observation that most of the movies of the 1930s were escapist diversions for people seeking distraction from the daily struggle for survival. Fortunately, the trend is away from the superficial toward analyses with substance and subtlety.

My thesis that the movies educate while entertaining represents one perspective or one means for more deeply exploring the larger subject. The thesis itself is not original, but my elaboration of it and the premium I place on the instructional aspects of the movies are unique. Later discussions of some of the methods available for teaching with the movies will present opportunities to examine some of the skills useful in assessing the interrelationship between the movies and society. But before moving to an explanation of my thesis or a description of pedagogical methodologies, it is essential to appreciate what has been going on in film study. Even those whose interest in the movies is exclusively for their classroom utility will discover a need for some background. Like anything else, motion pictures cannot be treated in a vacuum; a fundamental understanding of the basics of their history and development as an entertainment medium, as an industry, as an instructional force, and as a means of communication is necessary before one attempts to teach with them.

For those who are unfamiliar, the way the movies have been examined may appear at first glance to be fragmentary and disjointed. Film study has yet to become a cohesive, independent field, continuing instead to be a composite of various subgroups from other disciplines. That circumstance is not likely to change in the foreseeable future and the impression of disorganization will remain. Furthermore, film study has followed the well-trod academic paths of specialization and categorization; compartmentalizing is a by-product of the successful effort to extricate film study from the clutches of the "buffs" and to establish it as intellectually worthwhile. The volume of literature is expanding geometrically, and trying to remain current can be overwhelming. Happily, along with the outpouring of monographs, there are complementary movements in the direction of interdisciplinary approaches and toward syntheses of what has been done. The results of these more general, more academically oriented analyses are more satisfying than previous ventures intended for coffee tables and vicarious consumption.

Someone whose attraction to the movies is for their pedagogical usefulness may fairly ask whether it is necessary to become expert in a second field. Some would unhesitatingly say yes for the same reasons they would insist that social historians be trained in demography or that students of the Constitution be schooled in law. I do not subscribe to that kind of thinking, although my own activity has so expanded that I always feel a desire to know more about all facets of the movies. Watching movies can whet the appetite for more, and teaching with them can stimulate a desire to know and understand them better.

A reasonable position is to recognize that while expertise is not required, a minimum level of proficiency is. Enjoying the movies, a common motivation for organizing a film-based course, is a good start. The familiarity obtained from years of viewing can provide a basis on which to build. The energetic novice can reach a modest level of proficiency without wading through innumerable specialized tracts which have only marginal utility. The best place to begin coping with the maze of publications, especially for comprehending the interrelationship between the movies and American society, is to read what historians have been writing. Some exciting trends are surfacing, and they give promise of simplifying much of the complexity.

In *Media and Methods, An Anthology* (1976), editor Bill Nichols found it necessary to apologize for the slight coverage of film history in his selections. His opinion is that "there does not seem to be as much activity, at least innovative activity, in this area as there is in theory and methods." His complaint was directed at a tradition (from Benjamin Hampton's *A History of the Movies* [1931] through Arthur Knight's *The Liveliest Art* [1957] to Kevin Brownlow's *The Parade's Gone By* [1968]) which conceived of movie history as an encyclopedic compendium of produc-

tion data focusing on the dramatic and written by critics.
However, that blanket statement overlooks some important
deviations from the norm, such as I. C. Jarvie's *Movies and
Society* (1970) and David Manning White's and Richard
Averson's *The Celluloid Weapon: Social Comment in American Film* (1972), an extended sequel to Richard Dyer
McCann's provocative essay "The Problem Film in America" in his *Film and Society* (1964). It also ignores improve-
ments in "popular" history such as Andrew Dowdy's *The
Films of the Fifties, The American State of Mind* (1975),
originally published in 1973 under the title *Movies are Better Than Ever* (the title change appears designed to promote the book in more scholarly circles). More importantly,
Nichols was unaware of three volumes published simultaneously with his, books which revolutionized film history:
Robert Sklar's *Movie-Made America, A Social History of
the American Movies* (1975), Michael Wood's *America at
the Movies* (1976), and Garth Jowett's *Film, The Democratic
Art: A Social History of American Film* (1976).

A historian, a professor of English, and a specialist in
American studies respectively, Sklar, Wood, and Jowett
altered the nature of film history by providing it with the
larger social context that had been lacking. Interweaving
standard social science considerations such as politics,
economics, and cultural change with their interest in the
movies, they provided a conceptual framework in which
they advanced several new theses while synthesizing the
work of others. Neither narrowly specialized nor unman-
ageably encyclopedic, their publications possess an eclec-
tic quality that appeals to those at all levels of proficiency.
They are especially valuable for the novice. They offer
broad overviews within a meaningful context and yet provide sufficient subtlety and substance to be intellectually
comprehensible and satisfying. The veteran will find them
stimulating because of their disposition to take old material
and reshape it in the light of new perspectives.

The maturation of film history reflected in these generalist works is also evident in studies of integral units.
Lawrence H. Suid's mistitled book *Guts and Glory: Great*

American War Movies (1978) is a good illustration. Suid's examination and analysis of how Hollywood and the military have cooperated in the production of war movies from King Vidor's *The Big Parade* (1925) to Richard Attenborough's *A Bridge Too Far* (1977) demonstrates how those films have reflected the social milieu. His is not simply a buff's estimation of "great American war movies"; it is a revelation of how one type of film mirrors society's changing needs, interests, and aspirations. Similarly, *American History/American Film* (1979), edited by John O'Conner and Martin Jackson, presents a scholarly evaluation of fourteen productions, beginning with D. W. Griffith's *Way Down East* (1920), and how they represent the society that generated them. In both publications, as in the generalist studies, the premium is on treating the movies within the limits of a larger conceptual superstructure.

A more comprehensive example of the restructuring and reorientation of film history can be seen in reviews of blacks and the movies. An area that traditional movie historians had virtually ignored, the black experience has now been captured by Donald Bogle in *Toms, Coons, Mulattos, Mammies and Bucks: An Interpretive History of Blacks in American Films* (1973) and Daniel J. Leab in *From Sambo to Superspade: The Black Experience in Motion Pictures* (1975). Less extended but equally valuable is *Slow Fade to Black: The Negro in American Film, 1900-1942* (1977) by Thomas Cripps. The depth of coverage is such that the subject has been rendered definitively. The mutually reinforcing association of blacks, the movies, and society at large comes through in a way that makes each element more comprehensible and the total more than the sum of its parts.

Not every recent endeavor in film history has been successful, however. While perhaps well intentioned, some authors have surrendered their objectivity and lost sight of the overall context. Two explorations of women in the movies, *Popcorn Venus: Women, Movies and the American Dream* (1973) by Marjorie Rosen and *From Reverence to Rape: The Treatment of Women in the Movies* (1974) by

Molly Haskell, are marred by polemics and are more useful for "consciousness raising" than disclosing the complexities of a very important topic. *The Only Good Indian: The Hollywood Gospel* (1972), by Ralph and Natasha Frair, is another instance in which a significant subject was mutilated by authors more interested in condemning the movie industry for its sins than revealing the origin and impact of those sins.

A similar warning is in order concerning the outpouring of memoirs prompted by the sales of Frank Capra's *The Name Above the Title, An Autobiography* (1971). The availability of primary sources should complement secondary evaluations by historians, but they do not. Capra's memory has been found to be frequently in error, and those of his successors are also suspect. Such reminiscences as Charlton Heston's *The Actor's Life* (1978) and Joshua Logan's *Movie Stars, Real People and Me* (1978) dwell on the anecdotal and are more titillating than revealing. Apparently designed for the mass market, Hollywood memorabilia are at about the same stage as those coming out of Washington fifty years ago.

The directions in which film historians are moving—the dual track of synthesis and treatment of the movies within a contextual framework—are being duplicated in other disciplines, though not at quite as rapid a pace. But the results are encouraging. Harvey R. Greenborg's *The Movies on Your Mind: Film Classics on the Couch from Fellini to Frankenstein* (1975) shows what can be done from a psychological perspective, though Hugo Munsterberg's pioneering effort *The Film: A Psychological Study* (1916, reprinted 1970) remains exemplary. John Harrington's *Film and/as Literature* (1975) reveals the progress in that discipline since George Bluestone's *Novels into Film* (1957). Harrington's work is a collection of essays, a typical first step in the drive toward synthesis.

My bibliography will not be an attempt to catalog all that has been done in film study. Rather, I will identify those volumes that will enable a teacher to achieve a working level of proficiency. My focus will be directed toward understanding the interrelationship between the movies and American society and, as a consequence, better appreciating how the movies have acted as teachers during the last seventy-four years.

Whether Hollywood's features have acted as mirrors on the wall or as windows to the world, that is, whether they have reflected society and its concerns or indeed shaped them, is a "chicken and egg" question that defies simple solution. Many have wrestled with the dilemma in an attempt to resolve it, but the results of their efforts have been less than satisfactory. The major problem is that most studies have not confronted the issue directly. Rather than exploring the fundamental question in an unbiased way, the propensity has been to start with a partially formed assumption that the movies somehow do teach. That situation is largely the product of how most investigations are conceived. Most studies are sponsored by individuals or groups disturbed by some instance or pattern of viewer behavior. Their intention is not so much to determine whether the movies teach or even how they might teach; their disposition is to try to "prove" that movies have caused—that is, taught—a disturbing behavior. With that sort of motivation, it is exceedingly difficult to identify the instructional role that the movies actually do possess.

The best-known and most exhaustive attempt to grapple with the "chicken and egg" quandary was the Payne Fund study between 1929 and 1933. The foundation provided the Motion Picture Research Council with $200,000 to determine the degrees of influence and effect of the movies on children and adolescents. The goal was to provide "a broader understanding of the total effect at home and abroad of motion pictures." The results were published in twelve installments under the generic title of "Motion Pictures and Youth." Researchers concluded among other things that delinquent children went to the movies more often than their counterparts, but they were unable to demonstrate a cause-and-effect relationship between movie attendance and delinquency. They did determine that the movies were "educational" and that they might "conflict with other educational institutions." In short, they were unable to explain just how the chicken operated, though a working assumption of the study was that it functioned in some way.

The inability of the Payne Fund investigators to generate conclusive results did not prevent others from using the data to "prove" that the movies indeed were teachers and that they caused or taught nearly all of society's problems. That was what the journalist Henry James Forman did in *Our Movie-Made Children* (1933), an indictment which concluded that "the movies have had very harmful effects on children, especially in promoting crime and sexual license." Forman was rebutted by an industry friend, Raymond Moley, in *Are We Movie-Made?* (1938), a response that sought to defuse the issue by relying on Mortimer Adler's contention that social scientists could not and should not judge the moral or political consequences of an art form such as motion pictures.

Television has become a subject of the "chicken and egg" debate too, and largely for the same reason that the movies have. Distressed by the behavior of children— either too violent or too sedentary—many groups have assumed that television has caused or taught that behavior, and they have set out to prove it. The most celebrated investigation was conducted by the Surgeon General's office in the late 1960s. Three years, $2 million, and twenty-three separate studies later, there emerged a series of "preliminary and tentative" conclusions.

So long as the objective is to verify that either the movies or television is causing some kind of deviant behavior, there never will be an end to the "chicken and egg" debate. I also think that it is next to useless to try to uncover an immediate and personal cause-and-effect relationship between viewing films and subsequent actions. Human behavior is motivated by too many forces to ascribe to it a single cause, even if it be the most immediate and most visible one. Such research might solve a legal problem, such as when lawyers attempt to convince juries that their clients were the victims of premeditated violence by assailants who got their idea while watching movies or television programs. That narrow a focus, however, obscures more than it reveals and leaves the more important question unanswered. We need to move away from the confines of a one-to-one relationship and toward a better understanding of the interaction between the movies and society as a whole.

Most serious students of the "chicken and egg" question find it easiest to respond to it with a compromise. The compromise position accepts that the movies have both reflected society and its concerns as well as shaped them. Because it is easier to demonstrate—I hesitate to say prove —that the movies reflect the larger social milieu, film scholars generally prefer to emphasize that dimension. Specialized film historians, for example, do that. A convenient illustration is Andrew Bergman's *We're in the Money: Depression America and Its Films* (1971). Though not a particularly profound analyst, Bergman does a respectable job in demonstrating that the vast majority of the movies of the thirties reflected the public's desire for escape. His handling of the Busby Berkeley musical series *Gold Diggers* (1933-37) is well done in that regard. His assertion that the public vicariously identified with gangsters and envied them is aptly demonstrated in his evaluation of Mervyn Le Roy's *Little Caesar* (1931), William Wellman's *Public Enemy* (1931), and others.

More successful than Bergman is Kathryn Weibel, who devotes a chapter to the movies in *Mirror Mirror, Images of Women Reflected in Popular Culture* (1977). Her survey of filmic images of women is sound and not as shrill as that of some others who have wrestled with the subject. Historians whose principal interest is not necessarily the movies but who feel compelled to address them in some way also emphasize the reflective aspect. That is how John Morton Blum discusses wartime films in *V is for Victory: Politics and American Culture During World War II* (1976), as does William Manchester in *The Glory and the Dream: A Narrative History of America, 1932-1972* (1974).

An interesting expression of the compromise is afforded by Andrew Hacker:

> Hooked on the twice weekly habit, Americans of the 1920's through the 1940's reestimated their own possibilities through a window on a new kind of life. The movies succeeded because they showed people the next step they could take. Hollywood's decline was not due really to television or to the trek to the suburbs. Rather its job was done. No longer hicks or greenhorns, Americans no longer needed the Bijou.

Hacker's central thesis—that the movies were an instructional force prior to World War II—is a proposition that studio heads at the time and film scholars today find congenial. It is grounded in assumptions about the composition of theater audiences and what they discovered in the darkened halls. He believes that the movies between the world wars, to paraphrase Karl Marx, were an opiate for the masses. Appealing to the semiliterate and poorly educated, the masses rather than the classes, the movies helped immigrants assimilate, aided uprooted farmers in adjusting to urban life, and performed a host of other comparable functions. They did that by conveying images of the mainstream of American life. Few doubt that the masses went to the movies to be entertained, but most also agree that they left informed and educated. The movies simultaneously reflected the lifestyle and values of the middle class while they urged the masses to embrace them. Hacker's thesis concludes, by implication, that the educational role of the movies has been completed and that only the reflective aspect continues.

As in the case of the movies, students of television have begged the "chicken and egg" question with the halfway argument that it both reflects and shapes culture. For instance, Michael J. Robinson writes in *The Public Interest* (1977): "In the 1950's television was *reflective* of our social and political opinions, but by the 1960's it was an important *cause* of them." That is an opinion that Joe McGinnis, author of *The Selling of a President 1968* (1969), would agree with. In comparing Hacker and Robinson, it is noteworthy that the former perceives the movies evolving primarily from the role of teacher to that of reflector, while the latter sees television reversing the process. To be fair to both, one should not read them too literally in their distinction between the functions of their respective media; they would be quick to argue that they are assessing which role is dominant at any given time.

If pressed on the issue of teacher or reflector, most observers of television would say that the teaching element is the stronger of the two. Because television has been more pervasive in the lives of the citizenry and because exposure to television begins at a more tender age and becomes a constant habit that absorbs enormous amounts of time, the predilection is to assume that television is a much stronger pedagogical force than the movies. Most people do not attend movies until they are nearing adolescence, whereas they are introduced to the television set virtually from birth. By the time children enter the school system, they have amassed thousands of hours of television viewing and accumulated a vast storehouse of information, if not knowledge.

My concern with television is predominantly as a conduit for telecasting movies, but I am not inclined to disagree completely that television today is a more significant instructional medium in its general programming than are the movies. However, in the debate over which of the two is the stronger force, I would not want to lose sight of the more significant fact that both media teach. We need to know better what they are teaching and how the classroom competition can and should respond to their lessons. Rather than assailing the media because we do not like what they are teaching, or adopting the pseudo-intellectual position of the PTA that we should slay the messenger because we do not like its news, we would better serve our students by instructing them in how to develop a critical capacity with respect to the stream of information from the visual media.

I would not pretend to be capable of providing a definitive resolution to the "chicken and egg" controversy. But I prefer to take an approach to the dilemma that is different from what has previously been taken. My inclination is to endorse the compromise of simultaneity in this controversy, to accept the fact that the movies have reflected the needs, aspirations, and interests of society while they have also structured them. My acceptance of the compromise, however, incorporates some variations on the theme.

For one, I do not subscribe to the belief that either the instructional or reflective function has been more dominant at any special time. Those roles have always coexisted in harmony even if one was more obvious than the other. Hacker's thesis, for example, presumes that better-educated audiences since World War II are not as easily swayed by visual images. Yet education, especially when measured by years of school completed, does not in any way guarantee visual literacy. The average viewer today is no more capable of intellectually penetrating Hollywood's slick productions than his grandfather was the earlier and cruder presentations. Visual literacy has improved to the point that audiences can see through the last generation's movies, but it has not developed enough to master the current crop. Students in the seventies howl with laughter at the "obvious" misinformation about drugs in the 1930s propaganda feature *Reefer Madness*, while they succumb unquestioningly to similar misinstruction in Dennis Hopper's *Easy Rider* (1969). Visual literacy has remained one step behind the motion picture industry's ability to teach, with more sophisticated technology that distracts viewers from discerning the lessons. Experience has convinced me that students are as deficient in comprehending and interpreting visual expressions as they are with regard to print communications.

Second, in determining what the movies—and to a lesser degree television—have done in their role as teachers, I am not necessarily disturbed about the social desirability of what has been taught. Whether the movies have had a good or evil impact on the human condition is a value judgment that concerns me as a citizen but not as a scholar. Good or bad, the movies have taught a tremendous amount, and my primary activity is helping students become aware of what is taught. As a historian, I am interested in ascertaining the accuracy and authenticity of screen renditions, comparing the visual presentation with reality. Helping students understand what they have unconsciously been learning at the movies may encourage them to make personal evaluations. In the meantime, I prefer the position of intermediary, encouraging students to penetrate the movies' illusions of reality rather than be victimized by them.

Third, my appraisal of Hollywood the teacher is also at variance with many traditional perceptions as well as the contemporary legal posture. One tendency has been to assume that the film industry teaches only through what are euphemistically referred to as "message" movies and that the teaching has been successful only when one can demonstrate an immediate cause-and-effect relationship between a particular picture and a specific human action. More accurate and realistic is the opinion of C. M. White and Richard Averson "that all films—born as they are of a particular nexus of historical circumstances—contain social commentary," that is, messages or statements. Purely didactic productions are in a distinct minority because the business has usually adhered to the old saw "If you want to send a message, call Western Union!" The profit motive discourages producers and directors from producing pictures whose statements are so blatant as to cause controversy and thus diminish revenues. The furor and subsequent House Committee on Un-American Activities investigation brought on by Warner Brothers' portrayal of the Nazi menace in *Confession of a Nazi Spy* (1939) reaffirmed the belief that "message" films cause trouble. The financial disaster of Stanley Kramer's instructional trilogy about racism, nuclear holocaust, and freedom of speech (*The Defiant Ones* [1958], *On the Beach* [1959], and *Inherit the Wind* [1960] respectively) so hurt that independent producer/director that the next time he came near a controversial subject, racism in *Guess Who's Coming to*

Dinner? (1967), he did so with a delicacy that could offend only the most hardcore racist.

Studios and independents alike have always expressed a preference for the presumably "noninstructional" features that unite viewers, such movies as William Wyler's *Ben Hur* (1959), Robert Wise's *Sound of Music* (1965), or Stephen Spielberg's *Jaws* (1975). But to believe that audiences learn only through grossly didactic preachments is to underestimate the American public's susceptibility to visual persuasion. The learning process in theaters and living rooms is much more subtle and insidious, which Hacker realized had happened with previous generations.

My argument is that audiences are constantly learning new things and reaffirming old material each time they watch a movie. Most of what they absorb is digested unconsciously and ordinarily in small bits. But the cumulative effect is more significant than the occasional learning experience that rivets attention on something large and sweeping.

The dynamics of the cumulative process can be seen through the dozens of films about the Civil War experience that appeared between D. W. Griffith's epic *Birth of a Nation* in 1915 and Victor Fleming's *Gone With the Wind* in 1939. Those productions contributed greatly to changes in popular attitudes about one of this country's more important historical transformations. The television production "Roots" dramatically altered those attitudes and is a superb illustration of one of the rare instances when a single presentation can change what people have become accustomed to think. A brief but incisive survey of the cumulative effect of viewer learning is "How TV Treats Cancer" by Harry Waters (*Newsweek*, November 13, 1978). Waters analyzes several made-for-television movies, beginning with *Brian's Song* (1971), to demonstrate the repetition of misleading statements about cancer and how the disease affects people physically and emotionally. His examination of television's "Big C Cop-out" also includes a comparison of Edmund Golding's *Dark Victory* and Hollywood's treatments since 1939. I find it very encouraging that this kind of analysis should appear in the mass media; it is an assurance that others are trying to forewarn viewers about what they learn at the movies.

Audiences will balk when the movies hammer away at something if the entertainment element is lost in the process. That happened when Hollywood fought the cold war. Attempting to placate HUAC investigators, the industry cranked out a series of anticommunist diatribes, such as Leo McCarey's *My Son John* (1952) and Edward Ludwig's *Big Jim McClain* (1952). While offering repeated warnings about the communist threat, directors lost sight of the paramount importance of entertaining while educating. Viewers turned away by the thousands even though they agreed with the instructional lessons. In order to have people consciously or unconsciously respond to its messages, Hollywood found it necessary to attract them and keep them in the theaters with first-rate entertainment.

First-rate entertainment, however, can be conveyed in a variety of ways, including artistically second-rate productions. Film critics are just becoming aware of the enormous drawing power and phenomenal impact of what they have disdained as "B" pictures (see "Attack of the Killer 'B'," *Newsweek*, August 1, 1977). *American Graffiti* (1973) cost less than $1 million to produce, grossed over $50 million, and was seen by at least twenty million people. It spawned a top-rated television series, "Happy Days," and kindled popular interest in the 1950s. American International Pictures has prospered during the last twenty years by providing a steady diet of films with statements that pander to the values of the so-called Pepsi generation. Producer/director Don Siegel has shown a remarkable capacity for manipulating audiences with "B" productions, such as *Riot in Cell Block Eleven* (1945) and *Invasion of the Body Snatchers* (1956), as well as "A" features, such as *Dirty Harry* (1971) and *Charley Varrick* (1973). *Invasion of the Body Snatchers* is only one of the many 1950s science fiction films of artistically inferior quality that film scholars study as anticommunist allegories. Roger Corman and Russ Meyers are two other directors whose second-rate productions have been profitable and influential.

When screen statements are congenial because one agrees with them or, more importantly, because they are unfamiliar, the information is consumed with the ease of dining. If those messages are brought forward deftly, that is, with an emphasis on verisimilitude, viewers are unaware of what is happening to their minds. That occurs whether the theater is filled with intelligent or not so intelligent people, educated or uneducated. Because people consciously go to the movies to be entertained, to be distracted from their daily existence, whatever critical skills they may have in other areas are deactivated in theaters. It seems that the switch that turns the projector on turns those critical activities off.

Former newsman turned social critic Daniel Schorr has addressed "the phenomenon of tailored truth" and concludes that people are no better prepared or capable of escaping "fact-fiction" distortion now than they were in the past (see "The Danger of Blurring Fact and Fantasy," New York Times, August 6, 1977). Although Schorr exhibits a certain naiveté when he suggests that the "romanticizing of history" in the movies of his youth "made little difference," his commentary on today's situation is revealing. Paying tribute to the verisimilitude that many directors can create, he argues that the reality emerging from filmic renditions transcends literal reality. This, I think, is a perceptive and valid observation. Schorr rightly concludes that the ability of directors to achieve a sense of literal reality is such that "one had to concentrate to realize that NBC's 'Raid on Entebbe' was not a documentary," a form presumed to be thorough and objective.

I do not believe that most screen writers or directors normally envision themselves as teachers when they compose a script or shoot a film. Yet, regardless of what one may think of the *auteur* theory—that movies are a singular artistic creation of a director—filmmakers do not devote months to a production unless they have something to say. Those expressions may not be messages in a pedagogical sense, but producers, directors, and writers usually select a property and film it in a particular way in order to communicate certain ideas they have.

The transmission of ideas to the audience may be subtle and may require critical viewing and interpretive skills that not everyone possesses. That was the case when some members of the "Hollywood Ten" included what could be construed as procommunist propaganda in their wartime productions. Trying to bolster the indictment of the "Ten" for contempt of Congress, HUAC investigators looked vainly for objectionable statements. Poor visual literacy kept the investigators from recognizing the messages in John Howard Lawson's script for Zoltan Korda's *Sahara* (1943) or in Herbert Biberman's *The Master Race* (1944). Such conspiratorial activity is not the norm; more typical is that of Richard Attenborough, who chose to direct *A Bridge Too Far* because he wanted to offer his opinions about the futility of war.

Like audiences who unconsciously absorb information, filmmakers sometimes communicate ideas without fully realizing exactly what they are doing. Movies are not produced in a social vacuum. Like any work of art, they are influenced by social, cultural, political, and economic factors that cause their creators to express certain ideas and to do so in unique ways. Because academic instruction and on-the-job training emphasize the technical aspects of filmmaking, producers, writers, and directors do not tend to be as knowledgeable as they should be about how and what they are unconsciously communicating to the public. Viewers must also be alert to that and critically perceptive enough to recognize how the images on the screen and the messages they convey are a product of the current milieu. A good way to appreciate and compare the impact of societal and cultural factors is to compare original productions and their remakes, for instance, Elliott Nugent's *The Great Gatsby* (1949) versus the better-known version of 1973 or Don Siegel's 1950s *Invasion of the Body Snatchers* with the 1978 re-make that changed the original in substantive ways.

The assumption that learning takes place only when one can demonstrate an immediate cause-and-effect relationship between a movie and a specific human action defines learning much too narrowly, but that kind of educating does take place. Military recruiters reported for years that whenever John Wayne starred in a new war film, enlistments jumped. There was an instance in Vietnam when a soldier was killed while planting an explosive charge in a Vietcong bunker the same way Wayne had in a Japanese bunker in *The Sands of Iwo Jima* (1949). More typical are the audiences of Alan Pakula's *All the President's Men* (1976), who go away convinced that they know all about Watergate and its participants. Whether it affects their behavior immediately, such as how they vote, has never been explored. That it did influence their attitudes and opinions in a general way goes without saying, predisposing many to accept uncritically the televised docu-dramas "Washington: Behind Closed Doors" (1977) and "Blind Ambition" (1979) because they portrayed the same participants in a like manner. Reshowing those productions in years to come will do more to shape Richard M. Nixon's historical persona than any scholarly treatise on the subject. Also, as a classic statement of the activities of investigative reporters, *All the President's Men*, book and film, contributed to the upsurge in journalism school enrollments because impressionable undergraduates grasped the dramatic visuals as the incarnation of reality.

In suggesting that learning takes place while viewing, I am not in any way saying that what is learned is always significant, or that every movie is of equal importance as an instructional vehicle. Some productions contain very substantial amounts of information or misinformation, particularly historical epics from the age of D. W. Griffith's *Birth of a Nation* (1915) and *Intolerance* (1916) to Joseph Sargent's *MacArthur* (1977), produced by Frank McCarthy of *Patton* (1970) fame. But more often movies contain small bits and pieces of information, much of it inconsequential, and it is the cumulative process that can make otherwise insignificant imagery important. Seeing the same thing over and over again will eventually sway the doubtful as well as the ignorant. The portrayal of the lifestyle and behavior of the American Indian is a most obvious illustration of the power of the repetitive process. Small particles pile one on top of the other until viewers are convinced that they are knowledgeable about a subject.

What audiences learn of greater or lesser importance can be demonstrated through investigation of two movies, one very old, Griffith's *Birth of a Nation* (1915), and one of more recent vintage, Arthur Penn's *Bonnie and Clyde* (1967). I have selected these two because they were and continue to be shown frequently and because each director endeavored to be faithful to the facts in his re-creation of history.

Every film scholar finds it necessary at some time to deal with Griffith's *Birth of a Nation*. Generally acknowledged as the first great feature movie and the cinematic triumph of the master of the silent film, it probably has received more attention than any other picture. Teachers of film appreciation like to screen it to reveal the technical developments incorporated by Griffith and his cameraman Billy Bitzer. Traditional historians have also worked with it, as did Thomas Cripps in "The Negro Reaction to the Motion Picture 'Birth of a Nation' " (*Historian*, May 1963). Cripps investigated how the movie disturbed blacks and recorded the efforts of the NAACP and others to have it censored or banned.

While secretly assembling his motion picture, Griffith realized that he was making screen history, but he did not think that he was teaching history or anything else. Griffith's rendition of the Civil War and Reconstruction, adapted from Thomas Dixon's successful novel and play "The Clansman" (the film's original title until a later suggestion by Dixon), was identical to the version he had heard from his Confederate Army veteran father when growing up in Kentucky. It was also thematically similar to several other shorter movies that preceded it. The adverse public reaction by a small but vocal minority of blacks and white progressives startled and angered him, enough so that he published the pamphlet "Freedom of Speech in America" and decided to film *Intolerance* (1916) to answer his critics.

Griffith's instructional statements reinforced long-standing Southern attitudes on the Civil War, its aftermath, and the nature of the people involved. His portrayal of the Ku Klux Klan as a band of valiant Confederate veterans trying to save white womanhood from rapacious blacks and the white-dominated political system from ignorant and scheming blacks was convincing to many people. It was so persuasive that it is credited with stimulating a revival of the Klan at Stone Mountain, Georgia, in 1915 and helping to sustain the group's popularity for over a decade.

Among other historical factors and interpretations, he emphasized that the war needlessly pitted friend against friend, that Abraham Lincoln was a compassionate father figure and the only one who could have prevented vengeful reconstruction, that radical reconstruction was conducted by mulattoes and Negrophiles, not Republicans. In more general terms, he reaffirmed Southern beliefs that "good" blacks were dutiful house servants who knew their place, an image that would be perpetuated in hundreds of other productions, most notably *Gone With The Wind* (1939), in which Hattie McDaniel played the role of "Aunt Jemima" so convincingly that she received an Academy Award. Griffith also contributed to an image of white women as passive maternal figures who had to be protected from the lust of men, particularly black men.

If *Birth of a Nation* had been distributed exclusively south of the Mason-Dixon line, it would never have transcended a role of reflecting social attitudes. However, it was enormously popular elsewhere in the country, and there it taught audiences to accept what previously had been contrary to its beliefs. In this regard, the time of the appearance of Griffith's epic becomes crucial. White Northern attitudes toward blacks—and consequently the Civil War experience—was in flux in 1915. The Grand Army of the Republic, the Union veteran's organization that waved the "bloody shirt" of rebellion at every election, was a relic of the past, and a southern Democrat, Woodrow Wilson, was in the White House. Furthermore, the once glorious war to free the slaves did not seem so noble to recently arrived immigrants who competed with blacks for jobs and housing. The previous twenty years had witnessed a massive internal migration of blacks from the rural South to the industrial cities of the East and Midwest, where they challenged the white working class in the marketplace. Educated people who were captivated by the new pseudo-science of eugenics looked at Griffith's portrayal of blacks and found it comparable to the writings of Madison Grant, *The Passing of the Great Race* (1916), and others. Politicians trying to rule brown and yellow people in America's new overseas empire from Panama to the Philippines were having second thoughts about traditional Southern attitudes toward nonwhites. Because of the Jim Crow laws of the 1890s, few blacks voted; the Republican party was more interested in attracting Southern whites to the GOP and had long since shelved its protectionist approach toward blacks. Under these circumstances, it was not difficult for Griffith to persuade (teach) people that his rendition was accurate. His visual re-creation provided non-Southerners with reasons for justifying latent racist attitudes that were in the process of erupting. As well as contributing to a revival of the Klan, *Birth of a Nation* also had a part in a furious round of racial confrontations in Chicago, East St. Louis, and elsewhere.

While communicating his Southern viewpoint throughout Northern cities, Griffith was unwittingly popularizing a new school of historical interpretation. A decade earlier, William A. Dunning in *Reconstruction, Political and Economic* (1907) launched a reevaluation of the events of the immediate post-Civil-War period. Dozens of monographs followed, culminating in Claude G. Bowers' *The Tragic Era* (1929). Dunning was partially responsible for prompting the revisionist work of Ulrich B. Phillips, whose *American Negro Slavery* (1918) painted a picture of blacks and slavery that was exactly opposite that of the abolitionists and nineteenth-century historians. *Birth of a Nation* sped what would have otherwise been a slow process of public awareness of the historical scholarship and helped pave the way for the acceptance of what Phillips and others like him would write. When President Wilson, a historian as well as a politician, purportedly described the movie as "history written in lightning," he was verifying that Griffith's lessons were compatible with the "best" history of the day. What Griffith taught to Northern audiences and reaffirmed for Southern ones may seem preposterous today in light of later historical and filmic reinterpretations, but in 1915 the director's screen instruction was illuminating and, for his white viewers, ennobling. It would stand for thirty years and be repeated again and again in his own films, such as *Abraham Lincoln* (1930), and those of others, reaching a crescendo in *Gone With the Wind.*

There is no question that public willingness to accept Griffith's messages was directly related to sociopolitical factors that disposed viewers to be sympathetic to his rendering. That willingness was further enhanced by the movie's dramatic qualities. Technically, it was a sensational production: its verisimilitude and *mise-en-scène* (the aura emanating from details of setting, scenery, and staging) were overpowering. When the director tried to reinterpret the American Revolution for the sesquicentennial in *America* (1925), the sociopolitical elements necessary for making his reinterpretation congenial were missing. He had started the project at the urging of the Daughters of the American Revolution, but he wound up being criticized by them for distorting history. Some historians, notably Charles M. Andrews in *The Colonial Background of the American Revolution* (1924), were also endeavoring to reinterpret the revolutionary experience at that time, but their interpretations were so contradictory to the popular patriotic school that they never permeated the mass consciousness. *America* was not up to the technical and entertainment standards of *Birth of a Nation* either, and its illusion of reality was weak. The film drew small audiences, and Griffith's messages were ignored. The director never understood why *America* failed at the box office, largely because he did not appreciate the importance of conveying historical statements that either reaffirmed tradition or were part of a reinterpretation that audiences had been prepared to accept by other societal factors.

A different kind of instructional situation prevailed with Arthur Penn's *Bonnie and Clyde*. Warren Beatty produced the picture, starred as Clyde, purchased the script, and convinced Penn to direct it because he believed it a commercially valuable property. The producer and director were impressed by the "outlaw" quality of the Depression-era gangster and thought it would be appealing. By 1967 the backbone of the film industry was viewers in the seventeen-to-thirty age bracket. That was the group that was rebelling against everything in the 1960s, from middle class social conventions to the war in Vietnam, and styled itself as the "counter-culture." Penn and Beatty were convinced that if they could get audiences to identify vicariously with Bonnie and Clyde they would make a fortune.

Knowing that nearly everyone had heard of Bonnie and Clyde but that hardly anyone knew what they looked like, they began by casting physically attractive people and costuming them fashionably. The public's ignorance of the biographical essentials of the protagonists made it possible to construct virtually any story line, and the narrative offered a number of statements that took advantage of that ignorance. Penn's Bonnie and Clyde became folk heroes for the dispossessed of the Depression: their life of crime was directed against the banks that had unmercifully driven farmers from their land. Sharing with these people, Bonnie and Clyde were projected as latter-day Robin Hoods. They were not really criminals in the usual sense. The path that had led them to confront the system was strewn with chance circumstances. They had not chosen a criminal existence; rather, they stumbled into one and were continually searching for ways to escape it. The forces of law and order were brutal and vengeful and did not understand the two. Those forces proceeded to annihilate Bonnie and Clyde in a seemingly unending fusillade that elicited sympathetic and compassionate responses from the viewers.

Youthful audiences reacted enthusiastically to that

imagery. Bonnie and Clyde's symbolic destruction of a bank that failed came across as an act of civil disobedience not unlike those of antiwar protesters in wrecking Selective Service offices. The general attack on the "system" also appealed to black audiences, a phenomenom that startled Penn, since he had not anticipated it. Frank Hamer, the Texas Ranger who hunted down Bonnie and Clyde, could easily be seen as an expression of establishment repression in the 1960s as well as the 1930s, a cross between the Sheriff of Nottingham and Lyndon Johnson. When Penn included in the picture a flying chunk of skull to represent the head of Clyde during his death throes, he was drawing a conscious parallel to the assassination of John F. Kennedy, the existential hero of America's alienated youth.

Prostituting history to lionize Bonnie and Clyde as antiestablishment heroes was denounced by the pillars of the status quo. The dean of American movie critics, Bosley Crowther of the *New York Times*, condemned the picture as a "deliberately buffoonized" miscarriage of history, "a cheating with the bare and ugly truth." One of the few experts on the subject, John Toland, published a rejoinder, "Sad Ballad of Bonnie and Clyde" (*New York Times Magazine*, February 9, 1968). Those attacks were rebutted by a younger generation of film critics who took it on themselves to defend the picture's historical accuracy. *Bonnie and Clyde* to them was a "documentary of a kind," "a W.P.A. mural of the thirties," and a film that made one feel he was "actually witnessing history." This last comment was a testimony to the verisimilitude that Penn produced. He and the screenwriters had labored to develop a convincing illusion of reality, and they had succeeded. However, it should be emphasized that doing so was not all that difficult because so few people had any significant acquaintance with what was being portrayed; proper costuming and renting automobiles from the period were practically enough, given audience ignorance. A few artifacts formed an ambiance in which a convincing and compelling narrative would be believed because viewers were very willing to do so at the time.

The debate on the film's use or misuse of history was lost on the millions who rushed to clothe themselves like Bonnie or Clyde and who made its musical theme a hit record. More importantly, they did not want to know what was "right." Much as the lessons of Griffith had reinforced latent racist feelings, the messages of Penn and Beatty ennobled the behavior of the Chicago Seven, the Catonsville Nine, and millions of other confrontations with the establishment. Penn's statements in defense of the criminal duo were embraced by people who wanted their actions defended and thus identified with the anti-heroes.

Penn duplicated his instructional triumph in *Little Big Man* (1970). This time the subject was the American Indian, and the director proceeded to reinterpret history, especially what had been generally taught in the movies. His success in convincing viewers of his message concerning Indians as "human beings," tolerant, peace-loving victims of white greed, was achieved in the same way Griffith's success was in *Birth of a Nation*. Popular attitudes about Indians were in a state of flux. The "Red Power" movement was pressuring historians and filmmakers to revise old interpretations and images. Audiences, at least youthful ones, had been prepared by the best-selling *Bury My Heart at Wounded Knee* (1970) by Dee Brown and *Custer Died for Your Sins, An Indian Manifesto* (1969) by Vine Deloria, Jr. to accept new screen messages. Sociopolitical factors had shaped a milieu in which *Little Big Man* sped the process of historical revision. Today, at the movies and on television, it is obligatory to show the American Indian as the "noble savage" or the ecologically minded "child of nature," stereotypes no more valid than the previous one.

INTERPRETING THE LESSONS OF THE MOVIES

Discovering, examining, and evaluating what the movies teach is a process quite comparable to literary criticism. Movies can be construed as documents that are subject to scrutiny from a variety of angles. Furthermore, the same production can be subjected to analysis by various disciplines according to the particular concerns and perspectives of each.

Good movies, like good literature, lend themselves to multifaceted and multilevel interpretations. However, the interpretive process is a mixture of objective and subjective considerations, and moderation is advisable. Elia Kazan's Academy Award-winning *On the Waterfront* (1954) is a useful illustration of a film that can be analyzed from several vantage points. The principal message is usually identified as a warning that mobsters and organized crime are infiltrating the longshoreman's union. An unidentified government body is trying to block that infiltration; but it can only do that, Kazan tells audiences, if citizens cooperate by testifying. The message is self-evident to even the least perceptive viewers and can be compared to other less than subtle warnings of the threat of organized crime, such as Mark Robson's *The Harder They Fall* (1956), an exposé of corruption in professional boxing.

As a reflection of its social milieu, *On the Waterfront* can be seen as a by-product of the famous 1950 Kefauver Committee investigation into criminal syndicates, an investigation which when televised by a New York City independent channel became the nation's first popular daytime program. It can also be viewed as a stimulant of public interest in the relationship between organized crime and labor unions and thus instrumental in the creation in 1956 of a special Senate committee, the McClellan Committee, to examine that association. More importantly, the visual portrayal in *On the Waterfront* contributed to the American Federation of Labor's decision in late 1954 to expel the International Longshoreman's Association for refusing to rid itself of the racketeering elements.

To stop at this point would be to miss an important message or statement by Kazan. *On the Waterfront* can be interpreted as justifying the actions of an informer, behavior generally considered by society as distasteful at best and often condemned, as was done by John Ford in *The*

Informer (1935). More specifically, the picture can be taken as an apologia by Kazan to explain his favorable testimony before HUAC. The director had testified in 1952 against his associates who were fellow travelers in the Communist party of America, and his film has been interpreted as his attempt to demonstrate the morality of his actions. Most audiences probably grasped Kazan's argument on behalf of informers but would not have been aware of its full implications because of their unfamiliarity with the director's life.

Most movies lack the interpretive richness of an *On the Waterfront*, and thousands can be searched futilely for anything substantial. Fredrick de Cordova's *Bedtime for Bonzo* (1951), a Ronald Reagan vehicle, and its sequel, *Bonzo Goes to College* (1952), are examples of productions with no redeeming interpretive value, but which have become famous because of Johnny Carson's frequent references when chiding de Cordova, his producer. The majority fall somewhere between the extremes, and it is necessary to have a good idea of what is available. The question most often asked of me is, What movies are available that address a certain subject? I have met several teachers who have accidentally stumbled across a distributor's catalog, usually Macmillan-Audio-Brandon Films because of its wide distribution, and have erroneously concluded that this product line is the only one available. Nearly every movie made since the introduction of celluloid safety stock in 1948 can be rented, as well as many made before that date, though the number decreases as one goes further back in time. Unfortunately, very few from the silent era remain, and those that do tend to be the "classics."

A BRIEF SURVEY OF SOME AVAILABLE FILMS

I would now like to briefly survey some of the feature films in the rental marketplace that possess an interpretive usefulness. My focus is on the more recent material, those movies from the last twenty years, because these are the ones that the average individual has watched and the ones that have helped educate him. There is also a greater variety in the pictures of this recent era because of the ascendancy of independent producer-directors with a "try anything once" philosophy. Certain genres are always with us, and formula films rise and fall in popularity as filmmakers imitate the latest successful type; but the demise of the studio system and its centralizing tendencies has generated a continuing diversity. This survey, however, is only a suggested introduction that can be readily extended.

Historians of virtually every historical period and section of the world will find that Hollywood has had something to say about their particular interest. The industry's willingness to address non-American themes is a result of the ever-growing importance of the international market. Since World War II, producers have been concerned with properties that will appeal worldwide, because the foreign box-office returns have increased enough to reach a par with domestic receipts. That concern was first manifested in the early 1950s, when the high cost of Cinemascope and its wide-screen imitators prompted Hollywood to reexamine the ancient world. The first was Henry Koster's *The Robe* (1953) and was quickly followed by a sequel, Delmer Daves' *Demetrius and the Gladiators* (1954), Cecil B. DeMille's remake of *The Ten Commandments* (1956), and new renditions of *Ben Hur* (1959) by William Wyler and *King of Kings* (1961) by Nicholas Ray. All of them touch upon Judaeo-Christian religious themes as well as reveal screen images of life during the Roman dynasty. They can be complemented with Mervyn LeRoy's *Quo Vadis* (1951), Stanley Kubrick's *Spartacus* (1960), Richard Fleischer's *Barabbas* (1962), and George Stevens' *The Greatest Story Ever Told* (1965), in addition to the more secular-oriented *Julius Caesar* (1954) by Joseph Mankiewicz, *Alexander the Great* (1956) by Robert Rossen, and *The Fall of the Roman Empire* (1964) by Anthony Mann. Nearly all were lavish spectacles with ample amounts of sex and sadism. "Exposing" the ancient world has been a time-honored method used by Hollywood to evade the censors; it reached its nadir with Joseph L. Mankiewicz's *Cleopatra* (1963).

The middle period in recorded history has also been probed by writers and directors in search of desirable properties. Beginning with MGM's first wide-screen effort, *Knights of the Round Table* (1953) by Kevin Hughes, Hollywood has portrayed the Dark Ages from medieval Normandy in Franklin Schaffner's *The War Lord* (1965), to England and its royal families in Peter Glenville's *Becket* (1964) and Anthony Harvey's *Lion in Winter* (1968), to seafaring Norsemen in Richard Fleischer's *The Vikings* (1958) and Jack Cardiff's *The Long Sleep* (1964). The modern world emerged in Carol Reed's *The Agony and the Ecstasy* (1965), Fred Zinnemann's *A Man for All Seasons* (1966), and Kevin Hughes' *Cromwell* (1970). The list of productions is not as long as that for the ancient world, but the same tendency to sensationalize remains. Great exertions are made at authenticating locale and costume—*The Lion in Winter* is outstanding in that regard—only to be undermined by one-dimensional stereotyping of the individuals and issues.

The most exhaustive attention has been devoted to the contemporary world, especially in genre films. John Ford's trilogy—*Fort Apache* (1948), *She Wore a Yellow Ribbon* (1949), and *Rio Grande* (1950)—helped rescue the moribund western and lay the foundation for its maturation into the adult variety. Beginning with Howard Hawks' *Red River* (1948) and continuing with Fred Zinnemann's *High Noon* (1952), George Stevens' *Shane* (1953), and Anthony Mann's *The Man From Laramie* (1955), America's westward expansion was treated with subtlety and a degree of sophistication. The western remains primarily a vehicle for action and adventure, but many examples of the genre, such as Tom Gries' *Will Penny* (1968), Abraham Polonsky's *Tell Them Willie Boy is Here* (1969), and Edwin Sherin's *Valdez is Coming* (1971), have reeducated audiences with exposure to a more variegated western experience.

War movies have also matured as a genre in the last thirty years, and they reveal as much about America's military exploits as they do about the society that gave birth to them. They reappeared in 1948-49—Sam Wood's *Command Decision*, Delmer Daves' *Task Force*, and Dore Schary's *Battleground*—and have thrived ever since. Some thought that the controversy surrounding the war in Vietnam would fatally undermine the genre, but after a brief hiatus in the late 1960s, war movies have returned with a vengeance, including Richard Fleischer's *Midway* (1976), Richard Attenborough's *A Bridge Too Far* (1977), and Joseph Sargent's *MacArthur* (1977). And now that the war in Vietnam has become a part of history, it too is spawning visual portrayals, including Hal Ashby's *Coming Home*, *The Boys from Company C*, and Michael Cimino's *The Deerhunter*, all made in 1978, with Francis Ford Coppola's *Apocalypse Now* (1979) the ultimate extravaganza. Like the western, war movies exist essentially as vehicles for action and adventure, but they also have matured into an adult version. Such themes as "war is hell"—Darryl F. Zanuck's *The Longest Day* (1962) and Carl Foreman's *The Victors* (1963)—and a questioning of the competence and loyalty of military leaders—Otto Preminger's *The Court Martial of Billy Mitchell* (1955), Stanley Kubrick's *Paths of Glory* (1958), and John Frankenheimer's *Seven Days in May* (1963)—have been pursued with success. Other facets of contemporary life portrayed by Hollywood that are of interest to historians may be of more immediate concern to those in other disciplines and can be addressed accordingly.

Political scientists will find that the movies of the last thirty years have covered a good deal of the range of politics, but they are not overly abundant because political themes are of little value in the international market. In the studio era of the thirties and before, politics was taboo because any treatment would presumably offend certain segments of the potential audience. Exhibitors long ago concluded that political discussions could kill a film at the box office. Fear of government-imposed censorship also prompted Hollywood to avoid subject matter that might displease politicians. The films of Frank Capra, *Mr. Smith Goes to Wash-*

ington (1939), *Meet Joe Doe* (1941), and *The State of the Union* (1948), while successful, were atypical and generated few imitations. In most instances, politics was addressed indirectly within a historical context. Biographies of famous persons were the most common since the studios preferred those figures whose partisan identity had diminished with the passage of time. Screen presentations of Abraham Lincoln, whether D. W. Griffith's *Abraham Lincoln* (1930), John Ford's *Young Mr. Lincoln* (1939), or John Cromwell's *Abe Lincoln in Illinois* (1940), are illustrative of that tendency.

Robert Rossen broke with convention in his adaptation of Robert Penn Warren's novel *All the King's Men* (1949), a thinly disguised portrait of Huey Long. That he achieved heights of critical acclaim, the Academy Award, and the New York Film Critics Award for best picture of the year was remarkable. His principal message of demagoguery and the corrupting nature of politics became an oft-repeated theme, as in Raoul Walsh's *Lion in the Streets* (1953), another exposé of Huey Long. Revelation of the seamy side of politics was continued by Otto Preminger in *Advise and Consent* (1962), with the setting the United States Senate and the villain another Southerner. Both Preminger's film and Franklin Schaffner's *The Best Man* (1964) articulated another of Rossen's perspectives: politicians function according to an end-justifies-the-means philosophy. John Frankenheimer added a surreal dimension to that message in *The Manchurian Candidate* (1962), a macabre tale of international intrigue, mind control, and unscrupulous politicians. Frankenheimer repeated his warning about the possibilities of a right-wing coup d'etat in *Seven Days in May* (1963), as did Stuart Rosenberg in *WUSA* (1970). Rosenberg's story of a superpatriotic radio station owner who manipulates the public to gain his political goals is in many ways an update of *Meet John Doe,* in which a newspaper publisher is the manipulator. The theme that the public is misled by political charlatans was examined by Michael Ritchie in *The Candidate* (1972). The apex of the antipolitics political film was Alan Pakula's *All* the President's Men (1976), a movie that exceeded the financial rewards of All the King's Men while completing the circle begun by it.

There are not many political films with positive images and messages, and those that exist are stereotypically similar. Three stand out: John Ford's The Last Hurrah (1957), Melville Shavelson's Beau James (1957), and Dore Schary's Sunrise at Campobello (1960). Like Rossen, Ford filmed a best-seller, Edmund O'Connor's fictionalization of James Michael Curley, longtime mayor of Boston and governor of Massachusetts. But Ford set himself apart by focusing on local politics and by depicting the big-city boss and his methods in a favorable light. His populist message that boss politics was necessary because it benefited the masses instead of the classes cast a different light on the "ends-justify-the-means" attitude. His portrait of a fatherly boss with a twinkle in his eye confronted by a sanctimonious, self-serving elite sharply contrasted to textbook renditions, and the O'Connor-Ford reinterpretation inspired a scholarly reevaluation of urban machine politics. Beau James offered little more than The Last Hurrah, except to shift the scene to New York City and replace Curley with Mayor James Walker.

Sunrise at Campobello purports to be history written with a camera, though a hagiography of Franklin D. Roosevelt would be a more appropriate description. Writer-producer Dore Schary makes the point that although politics has its venal side, its practitioners can be honorable men and public service can be conducted ethically. Furthermore, political life can be compatible with the ethical and moral standards of a family man, an image also conveyed by Ford. By narrowing his focus to three years in the early political career of Roosevelt and ignoring the controversial New Deal period, Schary produced a picture comparable to those about Lincoln described earlier. In that context, something like the praiseworthy examination of John F. Kennedy's military service in Leslie Martinson's PT-109 (1963) could be construed as much a political as a war movie.

Sociologists will discover that Hollywood's legacy has been abundant. Whether the setting is historical or contemporary, filmmakers are attracted to making statements about society, its organization, operation, and value structure. In that regard, filmmakers act very much like novelists. For example, the conformity demanded by postindustrial society is challenged by Nunnally Johnson in *The Man in the Grey Flannel Suit* (1956), with the encouraging message that one can be caught up in the "system" and yet maintain his individuality. Less heartening is Frank Perry's *The Swimmer* (1968) or Mike Nichols' *The Graduate* (1967) with their themes of avoiding conformity by dropping out. John Frankenheimer reiterates the thesis that individuality within a different kind of system—prison—can be maintained in spite of the forces of conformity in *Birdman of Alcatraz* (1962), a proposition completely rejected by Stuart Rosenberg in *Cool Hand Luke* (1967).

In trying to cope with sociological issues during the last thirty years, Hollywood has been less a dream factory than a pulsating conscience. The social dilemmas of adolescents was framed within the motif of juvenile delinquency by Richard Brooks in *Blackboard Jungle* (1955) and Nicholas Ray in *Rebel Without a Cause* (1955). The latter was a devastating critique of the American family, concluding that maladjusted adolescents are a product of role reversals between fathers and mothers. Similarly, John Avildsen in *Joe* (1970) castigates both working-class and white-collar families for their inability or unwillingness to understand their counterculture children during the turbulent sixties. Elia Kazan has a more reasoned approach to addressing the problems of youth in his adaptation of William Inge's *Splendor in the Grass* (1961), as does Phillip Dunne in *Blue Denim* (1959), a discussion of teenage pregnancy. But not all productions by any means were serious in their perspective on adolescence. William Asher made a small fortune with his "beach party" series: *Beach Party* (1963), *Muscle Beach Party* (1964), *Bikini Beach* (1965), and so on. Juxtaposing the fun and frivolity of the beach parties with more serious endeavors is a revealing way of understanding how social factors shape film production.

No sociological issue has received more devoted and consistent treatment from filmmakers in the last thirty years than racism. Trying to educate society to be more tolerant of racial minorities—blacks and Indians mainly— has become fashionable in Hollywood's attempt to atone for its earlier negative stereotyping. Stanley Kramer's briefs on behalf of racial harmony are well known: *Home of the Brave* (1949), *Defiant Ones* (1958), and *Guess Who's Coming to Dinner?* (1967). Norman Jewison's *In the Heat of the Night* (1967) offered the message that blacks can be capable individuals, in fact more so sometimes than their white counterparts. Its sequel, Gordon Douglas' *They Call Me Mr. Tibbs* (1970), repeated that thesis. Sidney Poitier, star of all but one of these films, has built a career around parts as an extraordinary black man who reassures white viewers while acting as a role model for black ones. Any of his pictures can be used to demonstrate Hollywood's plea for racial harmony and its atonement for the images created by Bill "Bojangles" Robinson and Stepin Fetchit.

A sensitive and effective exposé of racism and its impact can be found in Robert Mulligan's adaptation of the Harper Lee novel *To Kill a Mockingbird* (1963). Aided by a better than average script, Mulligan was able to overcome the handicap of both liberal and conservative racial stereotyping inherent in most productions. His message of understanding resulting from calm, rational analysis did not ignite as much controversy at the box office as did more blatant statements, but the sophisticated presentation is compelling. Douglas Sirk's remake of the 1934 version of Fanny Hurst's novel *Imitation of Life* (1959) was also effective in its portrayal of a black girl trying to pass for white, the same theme that had been pursued in Elia Kazan's *Pinky* (1950). Finally, having felt that it had fully repented, Hollywood in 1970 began producing movies about blacks and for blacks that totally ignored pleas for racial harmony, for example, Ossie Davis's *Cotton Comes to Harlem* (1970) and Gordon Parks' *Shaft* (1972). The recognition of the financial power of black audiences was also instrumental in the film industry's shift to patronizing the black community. Unfortunately, it degenerated into what are sometimes termed "blaxploitation pics," such as William Crain's *Blacula* (1972) and others.

The process of promoting racial understanding and making amends for past sins has been even more deliberate in the case of American Indians. History of sorts was made in 1950 with the debut of *Broken Arrow* by Delmer Daves. The traditional image of the bloodthirsty savage was replaced by a portrait of the "child of nature" victimized by white society. That approach was continued by Sidney Salkow in *Sitting Bull* (1953), George Sherman in *Chief Crazy Horse* (1955), and Jesse Hibbs in *Walk the Proud Land* (1956). Each indicts the white power structure for its shameful treatment of Indians while articulating a plea for both improved race relations and better management of Indian affairs.

The apex of the film industry's attempts to undo the past came in John Ford's last western, *Cheyenne Autumn* (1964). The director, who admitted to having killed more Indians in his films than the United States Army had, believed it was time to reverse himself and compensate for past misrepresentations. His film of redress, like so many other handlings of racism, tended toward oversimplification of the issues. Elvis Presley also participated in the image change for Indians in Don Siegel's *Flaming Star* (1960), in which he played a half-breed trying to reconcile opposing forces, in Peter Tewksberry's *Stay Away Joe* (1968), and in Charles Warren's *Charro!* (1969). The trend toward cultivating a positive racial stereotype of Indians moved to the absurd in Arthur Penn's historical fantasy *Little Big Man* (1970) and Robert Altman's *Buffalo Bill and the Indians, or Sitting Bull's History Lesson* (1976).

Only a few productions, such as Elliot Silverstein's *A Man Called Horse* (1970), Richard Sarafian's *Man in the Wilderness* (1971), and Delbert Mann's *The Outsider* (1961), a story of the tragic struggle of an Indian war hero with alcoholism, exhibited a sincere attempt at an intelligent presentation. The dominant image to emerge in recent years is that of the Indian as a worthy adversary: Martin Ritt's *Hombre* (1967), Robert Mulligan's *The Stalking Moon* (1969), Robert Aldrich's *Ulzana's Raid* (1972), and Sydney Pollack's *Jeremiah Johnson* (1972). A valuable aid in following the changes in Indian portrayals is "The Indian in American Film: A Checklist of Popular Images of the Indian in the American Film" by Gretchen M. Battille and Charles L. P. Silet (*The Journal of Popular Film*, Vol. 5, No. 2).

If reality or accuracy is the standard of measure, few of the movies that address racism are any more authentic than most history films. Much of their value is to be gained from the indirect reflection of the social milieu they mirror. Second only to pornographic features, movies dealing with racism have generated more public outcry and indignation than any other type. Perhaps it is for that reason that Hollywood has virtually ignored anti-Semitism. Elia Kazan's well-known *Gentleman's Agreement* (1947) stands out as the single deliberation on that subject. The film industry has often been criticized for supposedly being dominated by Jews, and it may well be that studio heads like MGM's Louis B. Mayer and Paramount's Adolph Zuckor did not wish to draw additional attention to such a potentially explosive issue.

Psychologists interested in how the movies have functioned as an educational force will find that public awareness of human behavior and its determinants has been shaped by screen renditions. The functioning of the human mind has intrigued a great many directors, and psychological studies have been perennial favorites. John Huston, for instance, endeavored to explore the source of Sigmund Freud's theories in his biography *Freud* (1962). That severe trauma in childhood could lead to kleptomania, sexual repression, and hysteria is expressed in Robert Mulligan's *Fear Strikes Out* (1957) and Alfred Hitchcock's *Marnie* (1962). Phillip Leacock in *The War Lover* (1962) and David Miller in *Captain Newman, M.D.* (1963) are but two of dozens of directors who have pursued themes on the psychologically debilitating impact of war. The problem of schizophrenia is dealt with in Nunnally Johnson's *The Three Faces of Eve* (1957), Hugo Haas's *Lizzie* (1957), and Alfred Hitchcock's *Vertigo* (1958). Hitchock also observed in *Psycho* (1960) that an unhealthy attachment to one's mother could lead to psychosis. *Psycho*, of course, was essentially a horror film, a genre which has treated the dynamics of human motivation in the most unscientific manner, as in Roman Polanski's *Repulsion* (1965) and William Friedkin's *The Exorcist* (1973). Equally unscientific have been screen treatments of the causes and cures of amnesia, from Mervyn LeRoy's *Random Harvest* (1942) to Jack Smight's *The Third Day* (1965) and Edward Dmytryk's *Mirage* (1965).

Two notable excursions into psychology have dealt with behavior modification, John Frankenheimer's *The Manchurian Candidate* (1962) and Stanley Kubrick's *A Clockwork Orange* (1972). Both features offer an exaggerated image of how human actions can be modified by conditioning, and the results are meant to be frightening. The ingenious nature of the explanation may annoy followers of B. F. Skinner, but they represent a significant learning experience for those unfamiliar with the workings of the human mind. They are of interest additionally because of their commentary concerning the political overtones involved in such psychological experimentation. Warren Beatty in *The Paralax View* (1975), a thinly disguised allegory of the assassination of Robert F. Kennedy, also examines the subject of mind control and political violence.

Hollywood's psychological portrayals are likely to irritate professionals because of their disposition to sensationalize and to focus on deviant behavior. Ralph Nelson did that in *Charly* (1968), the story of a retarded man turned superbrain in a scientific experiment, and Martin Scorsese went even further in *Taxi Driver* (1976). Milos Forman's Academy Award-winning *One Flew Over the Cuckoo's Nest* (1976), a black comedy about life in a mental institution, is equally misleading and misinforming on the factual level. Possibly the worst illustrations of the film industry's continuing attempts to explain human motivation are the hundreds of crime and gangster pictures. Virtually all of them seek to explain what drove the criminal into his life of crime, and they usually conclude simplistically that chance circumstances were the fundamental causes. Pleas to better understand psychological dysfunction—Robert Fleischer's *Compulsion* (1958), a dramatization of the infamous Leopold and Loeb case of the 1920s, and Richard Brooks' *In Cold Blood* (1967)—do not counterbalance the prevalence of sensationalism.

Philosophy in general has not particularly captured the imagination of filmmakers; and, as the most popular art, the movies have not been inclined toward meaningful philosophical analysis. Their efforts in the philosophical vein have generally been discussions of ethics, and even these discussions have ordinarily been by indirection or implication rather than overt confrontation. For example, crime or gangster pictures have consistently raised questions about ethics, as have many movies about the political world. Criminals, police, and politicians continually confront ethical dilemmas, and the movie industry ordinarily portrays those dilemmas simplistically and the people who face them as one-dimensional and adhering to an end-justifies-the-means philosophy. That certainly is true of Mayor Skeffington in John Ford's *The Last Hurrah* (1957) and Sheriff Buford Pusser in *Walking Tall* (1975) and its two sequels. Tom Laughlin embedded that perspective in his *Billy Jack* series, and the same is true in the numerous "James Bond" escapades, *Dr. No* (1962), *From Russia With Love* (1963), and so on.

Interestingly, ethical quandaries have been dealt with most maturely and complexly in period pieces: Peter Glenville's *Becket* (1964), Fred Zinnemann's *A Man For All Seasons* (1966), and Stanley Kramer's *Judgment at Nuremberg* (1961). The first two are exceptional in that they discard the end-justifies-the-means posture and praise two individuals for sacrificing their lives on behalf of their ethical beliefs. Kramer's three-hour excursion into the question of personal responsibility for actions committed under orders is an example of the capacity of the medium for dealing with a complex issue. Kramer offers no easy answers or solutions, preferring to have his audience wrestle with the problem and draw its own conclusions.

More common are the simple responses to complex questions presented by J. Lee Thompson in the numerous ethical sequences in The Guns of Navarone (1961). Martin Ritt cynically asserts in The Spy Who Came in From the Cold (1965) that there is little if any discernible difference in the ethics of the "good guys" and the "bad guys." In a similar vein, Sidney Furie in The Ipcress File (1965) and Jack Cardiff in The Liquidator (1966) give the impression that any action done for the security of the state is ethical. Television, in dozens of police, private eye, and spy series during the last two decades, has more conspicuously sought to justify questionable or unethical behavior. The "Mission Impossible" series (1967-72) is the best example.

The least exploited of the liberal arts in the movies is economics. Taking to heart the disparaging description of economics as "the dismal science," filmmakers have avoided the subject. The little that has been filmed concentrates on the business world. The portrayals have been less than flattering and have no doubt contributed to negative student attitudes toward businessmen, a circumstance that annoys potential employers from the business community. An apt comparison can be made with politics, another subject shot through with unflattering images. The negative stereotyping dates from the Depression years of the thirties, when businessmen ranked dead last on the list of society's heroic figures. Edward Arnold made a steady living in those years portraying devious businessmen.

The heartlessness of the business world was castigated in Laslo Benedek's screen version of Arther Miller's play Death of a Salesman (1951). Robert Wise's Executive Suite (1954), Henry Koster's The Power and the Prize (1956), and Fiedler Cook's Patterns (1956) inspect the corporate structure, especially the struggle for power, and find few redeeming qualities. The same is true of Nunnally

Johnson's *The Man in the Grey Flannel Suit* (1956). The advertising industry is portrayed as a jungle in H. Bruce Humberstone's *Madison Avenue* (1962), and it is lampooned in Robert Downey's *Putney Swope* (1969). Mike Nichols' *The Graduate* (1967) and Billy Wilder's *The Apartment* (1960) further pilloried businessmen, and Blake Edwards' *Days of Wine and Roses* (1962) pictured alcoholism as a product of the business environment. Norman Jewison painted in a criminal dimension in *The Thomas Crown Affair* (1968), while the self-made man is satirized in Joseph Peuney's *Cash McCall* (1959) and ridiculed in George Stevens' *Giant* (1956). The most curious presentation of businessmen is that of Francis Ford Coppola in *The Godfather I* (1972) and *II* (1974); he depicts the dons of organized crime as businessmen rather than gangsters, the only difference between them and their legitimate counterparts being in the product line.

I have deliberately omitted a separate listing of movies that would fall into a category of literature. I did so for two reasons: first, the great preponderance of films—90 percent is a conservative estimate—are drawn from literary sources and consequently are appropriate for analysis by students of literature. Cataloging such an enormous list is well beyond my scope. My second reason devolves from the first. So much has already been written about the movies by students of literature that it would be difficult for me to make a substantive contribution.

The foregoing is meant to be a survey of some of the feature films the movie industry has produced during the last thirty years that are applicable to the liberal arts. The filmography is representative, not exhaustive, and ideally it will stimulate further investigation into what is available. Some 3,000 productions can be obtained, and I have mentioned only those with the most obvious correlations to academic disciplines. A worthwhile task would be to categorize all features according to primary discipline, the kind of thing students of film have done in detailing genres or types. If that were done, a system of cross-indexing could also be developed, for most movies have an applicability to more than one discipline, a fact well noted above in my frequent mention of the same production in the context of different disciplines.

THREE | FORMULATING A METHODOLOGY

THE TEACHER who closely follows some procedural steps
that I will enumerate can successfully use movies in the
classroom with ease and facility. Those measures have
thus far been discussed in general terms, with occasional
references to specific situations and circumstances. Background work is essential because academic ventures cannot be "seasoned" with a mere periodic interjection of a
movie, and also because teachers cannot function properly
without a preliminary framework. Moreover, the need to
develop a proficiency with both the raw materials and the
secondary literature should not be underestimated.

Completing the background preparation leads to a
crucial juncture with conceptualizing a framework. The
teacher must draw on all of his intellectual resources and
creative skills to determine his plans and discern how
movies can help him realize his intentions. I have already
identified one conceptual structure, perhaps the most
uncomplicated and universally adaptable—the examination, analysis, and evaluation of information and ideas
transmitted in films. The instructor uses the movies reflec-
tively, pitting his presentation against the filmic one in
either a comparative or contrasting manner. Students who
become familiar with the basic elements of the subject
through the teacher's introduction and supplementary

reading can evaluate what audiences are given to believe in terms of realism, authenticity, and accuracy.

To simplify matters—but with the repeated caution about confusing terminology—I call this conceptualizing process "documentarian," because the heart of the learning experience is the dissection of a movie considered as a multifaceted communicative document. Students in effect are scrutinizing a visual document in ways similar to their accustomed analyses of printed expressions. What I am describing is quite comparable in method to traditional literary criticism, the salient difference being that the focus of attention is on a movie rather than a book, and aesthetic considerations are secondary to the pedagogical thrust of the discipline involved. More sophisticated conceptualizations and techniques are available, but only exceptional students have the capacity for coping with them. The introduction of these should be postponed until one's audience has achieved a high level of visual literacy.

I consider the documentarian approach the most elementary and the easiest to adapt for several reasons. First, it can be used by any academic discipline: the same film or films can be investigated from a variety of perspectives and according to the needs and interests of each of the liberal arts. Second, it promotes flexibility: one can explore either a single production or a group devoted to the same subject. Conversely, individual or multiple themes can be pursued in one movie or several. Third, the teacher controls the total situation through the selection process: he chooses his own movies and they work for him to illustrate object lessons in accord with his goals. What happens is that one teaches *through* the movie; the film itself is not teaching anything per se. Topics can be dealt with either directly and on one level, or they can be tackled obliquely and interpretively. Fourth, the range of issues and the extent of coverage are limited only by the number of films, and thousands are available. The opportunity for free roaming is virtually limitless. Finally, the documentarian technique places a premium on versatility, which allows the instructor to use his imagination and to flow with events as his students reach higher interpretive levels. More narrowly focused methodologies can be confining, and that restrictive quality can lead to pressurized situations demanding more from the students than they can give.

The process begins by designing (conceptualizing) a unit or complete course intended to relay certain knowledge about and insights into a subject. One sets goals and selects motion pictures that are conducive to achieving those goals. At this stage, one does not have to consider the movies in any more detail than to identify them. The visual aspect should be temporarily set aside while planning focuses on how the predetermined goals can be accomplished with standard mechanisms of lectures and assigned readings. In that context, how the movies will be exploited should emerge from the instructor's pedagogical considerations. Too many novices start by selecting the movies and then proceeding to develop goals and accumulate collateral materials. That is commonly done because of a limited awareness of the raw materials and a tendency to use "favorite" movies even if they are not the best vehicles. Here the cart is in front of the horse, and chaos will result. Fitting the specific movies into the general framework rather than vice versa reduces digressions and makes the most of relevant material. Only after the unit or course has been fully shaped, its directions outlined, and its ultimate targets determined should significant thought be given to how specific movies are going to be integrated.

Within this documentarian method the movies can be engaged for purposes of comparison or contrast. Limited reinforcement of a subject is possible, but it is dangerous because so few Hollywood productions, in whole or in part, treat their subjects with fidelity. Contrast is the most likely and useful approach. After the students are fully versed in the subject, the filmic presentation with its information and messages can be thoroughly examined, analyzed, and evaluated. What the students gain will depend greatly on the instructor's own preparation, his capacity for film criticism, and his ability to lead his audience into fertile fields. Post-viewing discussion will center around the movie as it is carved into its component parts.

A variation is to show several movies on the same subject that have disparate points of view. Screening a number of different productions will reduce parroting and should prove more thought-provoking. Furthermore, choosing films of a similar nature but from various historical periods adds a second dimension. That is, the movies can be examined as microcosms of particular sociohistorical forces in addition to being expressions of directors and their collaborators. I suggested this type of approach earlier when I discussed the possibility of showing remakes of films; but it is equally valid in larger circumstances, for example, illustrating how changing public attitudes toward capital punishment affected the making of Michael Curtiz's *Angels With Dirty Faces* (1938), Robert Wise's *I Want To Live!* (1958), and Richard Brooks' *In Cold Blood* (1967). Regardless of the academic discipline being studied, it is almost impossible to bring movies into the classroom without alerting the spectators to some of the history surrounding the era in which the film was made. Similarly, some history of film must be taught for the students to achieve total comprehension and appreciation of what they are seeing.

Thus there is a dual function inherent in the documentarian technique which enhances its usefulness. On the one hand, students can assimilate and evaluate a feature's contents as the filmmaker's viewpoint, and then compare and contrast that expression with the viewpoint of the instructor or possibly other filmmakers. Because of this circumscribed usage and the absence of a larger context, students are learning in a situation that disregards time and place. Only the subject in question is relevant, and the film is treated as just another way of articulating a perspective. This narrow focus may be quite desirable if the teacher's intentions in showing the picture are limited and if only one or two movies are going to be screened during the course. It also poses minimal confusion for students who are being initiated into a novel way of both understanding film and grappling with alien subject matter. Incorporating general history and film history is time-consuming and of questionable value in such a situation.

On the other hand, students can study a movie as the product of a dialectic between the filmmaker and his environment. The information and messages assume deeper and more significant meanings within such a construction. As they address the needs, interests, and aspirations of society, directors and their collaborators function as representative types, acting on and reacting to their sociohistorical milieu. To provide such a format, one must show more than one production and engage in substantial historical discussions.

While still employing the documentarian approach, one can rearrange some of the steps and show the movie before preparing the students. This procedure is not uncommon, but it is hazardous. Many have done it out of ignorance, assuming that their audience is much more perceptive and talented than it is. But it can thrive with individuals of an independent mind who possess visual literacy, analytical skills, and considerable general knowledge. The teacher can crystallize his intentions and assist the students somewhat by distributing a list of questions for them to answer. During the discussion he can add his information and perspective to the analysis. The danger is that the verisimilitude of the visual portrayal, especially if it contrasts with what the instructor is attempting to convey, may foster misleading or erroneous impressions that are difficult to counter. That is a constant danger under any circumstance, and problems with visual literacy may require a reshowing if the comparative or contrasting exercises prove disappointing.

Formulating one's purposes and finding a method that stems from the documentarian approach presumes at all times that the movies are assistants or tools, not the principal object. Students, of course, may not recognize that fact and will resent more work than the simple viewing. Instructors who accommodate such an attitude, minimizing or disregarding lectures and readings, will soon learn that ad lib discussions dissolve into reciting trivia and the self-evident. Even in those courses where the movies are primary, such as "Film Appreciation" or "The Rhetoric of Film," students should be guided by skillful lecturing and carefully selected readings. There is no such thing as an entirely visual movie offering, and student preparation should be required to match that of the instructor.

Humanists and social scientists will find that the documentarian approach contains a great many variations and mutations. Much like the choice of readings, film selection can alter dramatically or ever so slightly the same course each semester. Also, growing familiarity with successive viewings of the same feature will reveal nuances and stimulate interpretive slants that instructors had not discovered the first time around. With each encounter, one will make adjustments and modifications until an individual or personal methodology emerges. I see the documentarian approach as an ideal starting point that can be modified according to the discipline and the teacher's preferences.

The definition and description of any methodology has a characteristic vagueness. While the mind may seek simplicity in generalizations, those can be frustratingly elusive and illusory. A case study of how one movie can be put to use in a number of liberal arts courses will help clarify ambiguities.

HIGH NOON: A DENOUEMENT
FOR A METHODOLOGY

I have chosen *High Noon* (1952) as a case study because it is applicable to several disciplines. Few films have such a remarkable affinity for all of the liberal arts, a factor that makes the leasing of movies less desirable than distributors would like. (Several distributors have introduced longtime lease arrangements, usually a year, with infinite showings as an alternative to one-shot rentals.) Several other films that an instructor might wish to lease or rent because of their suitability to many disciplines are:

Robert Rossen's *All the King's Men* (1949), Elia Kazan's *On the Waterfront* (1954), Fred Zinnemann's *A Man for All Seasons* (1966), and Francis Ford Coppola's *The Godfather* (1972).

High Noon was described by Arthur Knight in *Theatre Arts* as a "psychological western," a "movie filled with sharp psychological insights." *Saturday Review's* critic Hollis Alpert thought it full of "social significance," and Pauline Kael wrote in the *New Yorker* that it was "primer sociology." A lesson in "good citizenship" was the opinion of Phillip T. Hartung in *Commonweal*, an attitude shared by the anonymous reviewer for *Time*. Bosley Crowther of the *New York Times* and Bart Kass of *Catholic World* agreed that it was a drama of "moral courage," a film which asked the question, "Is a man conscience-bound to fight for the right when those he would save repudiate him?"

Of course, it was also recognized by all as a "historical" study, a portrayal of the Old West. That it broke with many of the conventions of the traditional Hollywood western caused mixed emotions comparable to those brought on by another genre film that forever altered the type, Arthur Penn's *Bonnie and Clyde* (1968). Robert Warshow ("The Westerner" in *The Immediate Experience* [1962]) perceived it as typical of the classic western, whereas Andrew Sarris (*The American Cinema* [1968]) dubbed it "the anti-populist, anti-western." D. M. White and R. Averson (*The Celluloid Weapon* [1972]) succinctly summarized matters: "Interpretations of *High Noon* (1952) are as numerous and differing as there are film critics." The same could be said of historians of the movie in later years.

On a more practical level, I chose *High Noon* because it is a creation with which most are familiar. Award-winning and popular over twenty-five years ago, it remains a staple of television. In selecting movies for the classroom, it is important to pick features with which one's audience is familiar, since they will then be more eager to watch. Also, if an instructor intends to screen a film as representative of a type or era or if he intends to demonstrate some kind of cause-and-effect relationship between the film and its social milieu, it is imperative to have one that was popular at the box office. No matter how great a teacher or the critics may deem a particular film, its classroom validity is seriously compromised if it was ignored by the public.

From the standpoint of preparing the students and giving them a standard of comparison, *High Noon* is useful because the screenplay is in print (Malvin Wald and Michael Werner, *Three Major Screenplays* [1972]), and the short story from which it was drawn, "The Tin Star" by John Cunningham, is also available. The important role that it has assumed in the evolution of the western genre, especially the appearance of the "adult western" and the many attempts to imitate it—Alfred Werker's *At Gunpoint* (1955), Delmer Daves' *3:10 to Yuma* (1957), and Michael Winner's *The Lawman* (1970), to name only three—has prompted considerable coverage in the secondary literature. One can consult George Fenin and William Everson, *The Western from the Silents to the Seventies* (1973) and Jim Kites, *Horizons West: Studies in the Authorship of the Western Film* (1970).

PLOT SUMMARY

A rule of thumb never to be ignored is that a teacher should not show a film which he has not seen before, regardless of any recommendations or reputations. Literary descriptions such as reviews can be misleading or misinterpreted, and even reading the screenplay leaves something to be desired. In addition, the instructor should have viewed the film recently and with course applicability in mind. Be careful of televised presentations because they are usually "edited for television" and there is no way of knowing what was cut. Finally, previewing the film shortly before exposing the students will enable the teacher to forewarn them as well as rekindle his own memory. When he finally shows it in class, he will not have to watch it carefully himself and can spend his time better gauging student response and caring for the equipment.

Preparing the audience is exceedingly important. Tell the students what they are going to see before showing it. Not only must one inform them about the subject matter, one must also introduce them to the movie itself. Various ways for acquainting students in advance and assisting them in the viewing process will be discussed later. However, a plot summary is a feasible beginning under any circumstance.

The public—and students are no exception—ignores screen credits in the same way that it avoids reading prefaces and introductions to books. Therefore, a plot summary should begin with the identification of the central figures in the production: director, Fred Zinnemann; producer, Stanley Kramer; writer, Carl Foreman; source of screenplay, adaptation of the short story "The Tin Star" by John Cunningham; and director of the musical score, Dimitri Tiomkin. The last identification may or may not be included, depending upon the role of music in the movie. In the same way, other elements such as special advisors or assistance in production should be noted as appropriate. The director's name is especially important, for its inclusion in the credits generally is designed to heighten credibility with viewers. Eventually, as students' awareness of film history is broadened and as they become more cognizant of the careers of the people behind the camera, the quality of their insights will be enriched and their capacity to make meaningful associations will be increased. Some background information, especially about directors and writers, could be incorporated. For instance, one could note that Carl Foreman was an active opponent of the House Un-American Activities Committee and was blacklisted shortly after *High Noon*, that Stanley Kramer was in 1952 ascending to the title of "Dean" of the message filmmakers of the fifties, and that Kramer and Foreman had worked together on four other films in the preceding three years as part of their own independent film company.

The cast of characters should be listed: Gary Cooper as Will Kane; Grace Kelly as Amy Fowler-Kane; Lloyd Bridges as Harvey Pell; Katy Juardo as Helen Ramierez;

Thomas Mitchell as Jonas Henderson; and Otto Kreuger as Percy Mettrick. The extent of the cast of characters is another individual decision. For this movie, one minor character who otherwise might be omitted is Samuel Fuller, played by James Millican. The part is small, but the choice of name is noteworthy for interpretive analysis. Samuel Fuller is a writer-director whose politics were at variance with Carl Foreman's, and the writer intended a subtle "inside" jab by using that name.

Finally, any information that might clarify the setting or give the action a context would be helpful. For *High Noon*, it is helpful to locate the place as Hadleyville, population around 400, in an unnamed territory, not a state. Identifying the date as 1870 or 1875 and briefly outlining what was happening in the country during that period assists in better comprehending the era. Students will be assaulted by so much detailed information within the narrative that any advance warning will be beneficial.

High Noon is an 85-minute movie whose action encompasses approximately that same time span, 10:40 a.m. to 12:15 p.m. The tension as the film moves toward its climax is unquestionably heightened by repeated glances at the clock and by having the audience and the actors moving in the same time frame. The story itself is in many ways a simple one, though each scene is calculated to probe a different issue and to resonate with its own message. The messages alternate between subtle and sophisticated and direct and uncomplicated, but the narrative structure is so clear and precise that viewers easily catch most of them.

The film opens with the wedding of an aging marshal, Will Kane, and his youthful bride, Amy Fowler. Kane is about to retire from his hazardous profession and become the proprietor of a general store in another community. Indeed, Amy's Quaker convictions, the result of the death of her father and brother in vigilante activity, require that Kane renounce his occupation. The ceremony is barely complete when the wedding party is informed that Frank Mitchell will arrive on the noon train. Mitchell, a murderer brought to justice by Kane, has been pardoned through some unknown political manipulations and is returning to exact his vengeance. Because Kane is no longer marshal and technically not responsible for the safety of the community, he is urged to leave immediately, which he does. However, a short way from town he concludes that fleeing is neither right nor expedient. Against Amy's protests, he returns. Failing to change Will's mind, Amy decides to go back to her family on the noon train. The judge who sentenced Mitchell also flees, telling Kane that he is a fool to stay because the town will not stand behind him.

Certain of the rightness of his decision, Kane determines to confront Mitchell and his three cronies, who have already arrived. His plan is to deputize the local citizenry to supplement his two-man force, one of whom is away transporting a prisoner. On learning the news, the other deputy, Harvey Pell, comes to the office and the two men discuss strategy. An argument ensues because Harvey is upset with Kane for failing to endorse him as marshal. Harvey believes that Kane is jealous of his liaison with Helen Ramirez, the marshal's one-time paramour. Harvey resigns in anger, leaving Kane alone.

Confident of community support, Kane attempts to organize a posse from among the men who had originally helped capture Frank Mitchell. One by one they refuse, and among the most cowardly is Samuel Fuller who sends his wife to tell Kane that he is not home. Only a sixteen-year-old boy, the town drunk, and Herb Baker volunteer. The marshal politely rejects the drunk and chases the boy home. He is thankful for Baker's aid, but the latter too will eventually stalk away when he learns that no one else is coming.

Failing to rally individuals, Kane goes to the church where Sunday services are being held. Interrupting, he requests assistance, and the service is transformed into a town meeting to discuss the impending calamity. The community offers a variety of reasons for avoiding a fight, and even the minister is equivocal. Those who impetuously think the marshal should be helped are cowed by the opinions of others. Kane is coming to realize that the judge's prediction was accurate. Fear and economic considerations blunt any public desire for a conflict with Frank Mitchell and his friends. What the marshal perceives in clear-cut moral and practical terms the townspeople view differently. Abandoned, he returns to his office, drafts his will, and prepares for the inevitable.

While Kane is conducting his fruitless search, the plot is complicated by a number of subplots, each with its own statement. The camera follows the missing deputy, Toby, as he brings his prisoner to Hadleyville. Beset by problems, he never arrives. Amy has a chance meeting with Helen Ramierez, who has also decided to leave on the train. Helen had been romantically involved with Frank Mitchell as well as with Will and Harvey. As the two women speak, Amy learns more of her husband's past; Helen also lectures her on the duties of a wife. In addition, Helen explains the difficulties of being a Mexican in an Anglo-Saxon community. The saloon is the location for several scenes as the men ponder the impending crisis and the owner makes ready for a celebration. Harvey Pell is a central figure in the saloon scenes: he is praised for the wisdom of his resignation, which irritates him, apparently because of a guilty conscience.

High Noon draws to its climax with a violent brawl in a stable between Will Kane and Harvey Pell. Harvey is trying to forcibly eject the marshal from the town. Besting Harvey, Kane goes to the barber shop for medication and then to meet the enemy. The gunfight is a protracted event. The four villains pursue the marshal through the town, and in the process Kane kills two of them. Suddenly, a third falls, shot in the back by Amy. At a crucial point Amy has abandoned her convictions and embraced the advice of Helen to be loyal to her husband. Now an active participant, Amy is taken hostage by Frank Mitchell, who drags her into the street. At the climactic moment she breaks free and her husband shoots Mitchell. A brief final scene shows Will and Amy boarding their wagon and leaving. Before departing, Kane drops his gunbelt to the ground and tosses his badge in the dust, grinding it with his heel.

The preceding is a sketchy overview of the narrative. Depending on the course and its purposes, it can be expanded to include other significant information. A political scientist may wish to amplify the description of the town meeting in the church or expand on the political intrigue that led to Mitchell's release. A psychologist would want to examine human motivation by identifying in more detail the reasons given by each individual for refusing to participate. A sociologist could extend Helen Ramierez' discussion of racial intolerance and associate it with treatment of other minorities in Hadleyville, such as Indians and the town drunk. Along with structuring the plot summary in keeping with one's needs and interests, the instructor should formulate a series of questions to be answered after viewing. This is essential to keep the students' attention focused on the predominant issues and to lay the foundation for an analytical discussion. The combination of a well-framed summary and thought-provoking questions will help compensate for visual literacy problems and will restrict student attention to essentials.

Beyond the teacher's plot distillation, students can be directed to read reviews. Most of those found in newspapers and periodicals have a summary quality and will supplement the instructor's efforts. They will also enable the students to better appreciate the reception given the movie by the critics and will acquaint them with several estimations of its value from an "artistic" point of view. Ideally, one should assign several reviews because of students' tendency to read one and assume that it is the last word on the subject. Some students realize that critics provide a subjective opinion and that they are not necessarily "correct" in their evaluation, but few realize that many observations by critics about the film's treatment of history, psychology, sociology, and the like are erroneous. Reviewers generally are trained in literature or the visual arts, and their expertise in other fields can be questionable. One may wish to require students to write their own critical analyses. If so, it will be necessary to teach them the difference between a summary review and something that is more analytical. Most newspaper and magazine reviews include a considerable amount of plot summary because their function largely is to assist readers in determining whether they wish to see the picture.

Excerpts from primary literature, autobiographies, or interviews during production can provide a wealth of information about the intentions of the filmmakers. Reminiscences of all species by movie personages are growing tremendously in popularity (see, for example, the *Newsweek* cover story "Telling It All: Memoirs of the Stars," January 15, 1979), but they are notoriously inaccurate and should not be included without first cross-checking the information. Unlike books, motion pictures do not incorporate explanatory introductions, and it is hard to discern how well the producers realized their intentions without reverting to printed sources. Trade magazines such as *Variety* and some newspapers like the *New York Times* commonly do feature articles and interviews around the time of a film's production or its premier, and they generally contain a wealth of information.

When possible, the prescreening preparation should include becoming familiar with evaluations by film scholars. These are available for *High Noon* and other significant movies. The Prentice-Hall series *Focus On . . .* is extremely valuable, for in addition to scholarly analysis its numbers usually include the screenplay, reviews, and other worthwhile materials. It is very unfortunate that the Prentice-Hall series has been discontinued, but many imitations are serviceable. Revealing this kind of information to the students, however, has the effect of doing everything for them, and I advise delaying its release until after the initial discussion. Independent research through library assignments can be a stimulating and fruitful adjunct for developing student skills.

ANALYTICAL AND INTERPRETIVE CONSIDERATIONS

The central core of the documentarian methodology is the examination, analysis, and evaluation of the information and ideas conveyed by the picture. The first stage is the identification of the major components; the second the process of interpretation. With thorough preparation and careful viewing, students should be able to assimilate most of the information and begin to comprehend the more obvious messages. At first, they will have difficulty recognizing the subtleties, but that will be less of a problem as they grow more familiar with the technique. More complicated and irritating will be teaching them how to separate the significant information and messages from the less important and how to organize a descending hierarchy. As mentioned previously, how well and in what ways the students interpret a film depends in large measure on the instructor's guidance and explanations. Some of the ways in which teachers from different disciplines can examine, analyze, and evaluate High Noon follow.

High Noon is ideal for the historian who wishes to familiarize his class with life in the Old West during the 1870s. Hadleyville is a community in transition somewhere between the edge of the frontier, Will Kane's ultimate destination, and fully developed civilization. One can evaluate the film's imagery against the historical descriptions of Frederick Jackson Turner, "The Significance of the Frontier in American History" (1893), Bayard Still's compilation of eyewitness accounts, The West: A Contemporary Account of the American Westward Expansion (1961), and Louis B. Wright's Life on the American Frontier (1968). It would also be helpful to consult Turner's The Frontier in American History (1920) and Walter Prescott Webb's The Great Plains (1931). Because Hadleyville is a maturing "urban" area, Robert Dykstra's The Cattle Towns (1970) is a convenient comparative standard, especially for the role and extent of violence and gunfighting. Dykstra's conclusions can be juxtaposed to the film's message that violence —the clash between the forces of law and order and the criminal element—was commonplace.

Determining the nature and quality of life in a western community will almost by definition require the study of the mythology that gave rise to movies like High Noon. Because the era of cattlemen and homesteaders has been over for nearly a century, and because the West is no longer a subject of considerable interest to historians, filmmakers have played an inordinately large part in educating Americans about this one facet of their heritage. (The Western era portrayed in the movies spanned a relatively short period, essentially the decade of the 1870s, and involved a small number of people; thus it is understandable that historians have not accorded it more extensive coverage.) Glamorizing life and perpetuating mythologies have been staples of Hollywood. John Ford spoke for the industry when he had a character in *The Man Who Shot Liberty Valance* (1962) comment: "When legend becomes fact, print the legend."

Some historians have tried to debunk the stereotypes created by Hollywood, for example, Henry Nash Smith in *Virgin Land, The American West as Symbol and Myth* (1957) and Joseph C. Rosa in *The Gunfighter: Man or Myth* (1969). *High Noon* has been called an "adult" western because of its effort at an authentic portrayal as opposed to the usual celluloid romanticizing, and because it deals with mature themes in a somewhat sophisticated way. Director Zinnemann tried to establish a credible aura by placing a premium on accuracy in setting, costuming, and special effects. His exteriors, with their emphasis on the primitive or crude nature of most western towns, can be compared with other "adult" westerns such as *Shane* (1953) by George Stevens and *Ride the High Country* (1962) by Sam Peckinpah, or they can be contrasted with the stylized illusion of *The Big Country* (1958) by William Wyler, *Butch Cassidy and the Sundance Kid* (1969) by George Roy Hill, and almost any feature starring John Wayne. Zinnemann's zeal for a lifelike rendition clearly shows the influence of postwar Italian neo-realism that was then fashionable in Hollywood.

Reflecting on the mythology of western existence as reinterpreted in *High Noon* and in the historical literature could include showing and discussing installments from any of a number of television westerns so popular during the 1950s, for example, the long-running "Gunsmoke" or the thinking man's western, "Have Gun Will Travel." One step further in the interpretive process would be viewing "The Real West" (1959), an NBC "Project 20" production that was designed to depict reality but wound up prolonging myths. The program is a compilation of stills that might have succeeded with a different narration, a problem easily remedied by someone who can substitute his own script.

Other subjects historians might want to approach in connection with *High Noon* include the extent and impact of violent behavior, popular drinking habits and the function of the saloon, the formation of transportation systems, and commercial business expansion. Kramer-Foreman-Zinnemann contend that violence was characteristic of early settlements and that its specter could arise at any time thereafter; that the saloon was the focal point of the community, a male establishment in which the consumption of large quantities of alcohol was the norm; that the stagecoach was rapidly made obsolete by the railroad; and that extensive, multifaceted business growth occurred in a relatively short period of time. In broader terms, those four elements are also integral to surveying the social and economic life of Hadleyville and countless other towns like it.

A political scientist or sociologist concerned with the evolution of the criminal justice system and political institutions in general will find several interpretive constructions in *High Noon*. The filmmakers inform the audience that police service was the most vital public agency provided by government. Consequently, the chief law enforcement officer, the marshal, is portrayed as the most prominent civic official because his responsibilities transcend all others. That imagery can be compared and contrasted with Dykstra's evaluation of law enforcement activities in *The Cattle Towns* and with Rosa's interpretations in *The Gunfighter*.

The circumstances of Hadleyville can also be paralleled with those of another emerging western town described in Theodore Brown's *Frontier Community: Kansas City to 1870* (1962) and can be compared in more general terms with Richard Wade's *The Urban Frontier* (1959). In-

vestigations into the development of police service in nineteenth-century eastern urban areas, Roger Lane's *Policing
the City: Boston, 1822-1855* (1967) and James F. Richardson's
The New York Police: Colonial Times to 1901 (1970), provide
a unique perspective on their western counterparts. In
something more of a sociological vein, though still pertinent
to the needs of political scientists, one could assess contemporary demands for law and order with the expectations of the citizenry in Hadleyville. It would be illuminating to study the logic of Mr. Sawyer, who laments:
"We've been paying good money right along for a marshal
and deputies. But the first time there's trouble, we got to
take care of it for ourselves! What we been paying for all of
this time?" Analysis of citizen responsibility during a community crisis can be approached with equal reward by
political scientists and sociologists. Finally, an exploration
of the controversial thesis of Edward C. Banfield in *The
Unheavenly City* (1968) can be applied to the Hadleyville of
High Noon in a most revealing way.

The paramount importance of law enforcement and its
executors as portrayed in *High Noon* has been the most
prevalent motif in Hollywood renderings of western frontier life. The information and messages of *High Noon* can
be placed in context by showing John Ford's *My Dar-
ling Clementine* (1946), Delmer Daves' *3:10 to Yuma* (1957),
John Sturges' *Gunfight at the OK Corral* (1957), and
Michael Winner's *Lawman* (1970). These are among the
hundreds that trace their heritage back to Edward L.
Cahn's *Law and Order* (1932) and earlier. Hollywood has
often expressed the opposite point of view too, and the
same topic can be dissected through analyses of films that
lionize the "bad guys," for example, Nicholas Ray's *The
True Story of Jesse James* (1957), Phillip Kaufman's *The
Great Northfield Minnesota Raid* (1957), and any of the 120
productions chronicling the exploits of Billy the Kid. Many
others provide a sympathetic image of outlaws, such
as Henry King's *The Gunfighter* (1950) and Arthur Penn's
The Left-Handed Gun (1958). John Huston's *The Life and
Times of Judge Roy Bean* (1972), essentially a remake of

William Wyler's *The Westerner* (1941), substitutes a ruthless judge for a marshal as the principal law enforcement official. Vigilantism has also been a popular theme.

As for the evolution of political institutions, *High Noon* suggests that civilization on the frontier meant the appearances of an administrative structure, a board of selectmen, and a justice of the peace. Yet it suggests that the New England heritage remains dominant, for in a time of conflict town-meeting democracy replaces elected officials. There is also an indication of elitism in the electoral process: leading economic figures hold all posts, and their opinions outweigh those of the common people. That portrayal can be assessed in light of the classic statement on the development of democracy in the West, Turner's "frontier thesis," and its numerous critics.

Filmic discussions of western political institutions beyond those involving law enforcement are scarce, because Hollywood has had a predilection for feudalism as the order of the day. Generally, the film industry has portrayed the West as politically unorganized and has asserted that the most affluent member of the community—there invariably is a dominant and domineering economic figure—rules it. Political organization is associated with urbanization, a development which comes only late to the West in Hollywood renditions. The pictures starring John Wayne are especially rich in creating an image of western barons, for instance, Andrew McLaglen's *Chisum* (1970) and Howard Hawk's *Rio Lobo* (1970), a remake of *Rio Bravo* (1959). The same theme is pursued in Edward Dmytryk's *Broken Lance* (1954) and Richard Sarafian's *The Man Who Loved Cat Dancing* (1973), and it is "modernized" in George Stevens' epic *Giant* (1956). A profitable way of researching the expansion of western political institutions would be to show one of these many motion pictures which envision the West as a collection of medieval baronies, asking why that message is set forth and how it stands against reality. Very often, a discussion of exclusions—what is not addressed in a movie, why something has been omitted, or why something else has been substituted—can generate as productive an analysis as that which focuses on inclusions.

Lesser concerns relevant to political science that arise in *High Noon* include public services other than law enforcement, urban areas as dependent subdivisions of large administrative units, and politics as subject to corruption. The film suggests that a town may establish other municipal services such as fire protection, that Hadleyville is subject to forces "up north" in the territorial government that can shape its future, and that Frank Mitchell's pardon was the product of political manipulation of an unsavory sort. The writer and director treat each of these issues as peripheral factors but ones that influence political decision making in the community. Student awareness of the authenticity of the imagery can lead to a better appreciation of the facets and phases of political maturation.

Pauline Kael called *High Noon* "primer sociology," an investigation of the responses of a community overcome by fear. Her sociologically grounded interpretation is expressive of the most common evaluations of the movie and in general terms epitomizes how a sociologist can use it well. Superficially, the production is a period piece, a western set a century ago. (A fascinating enterprise is to discuss what a western is, that is, what makes *High Noon* or any other movie a western other than costuming and set, and how the film's information and messages would be different if its setting were altered to the 1950s.) Screenwriter Foreman was quite conscious of a historical dimension, enlarging it within the screenplay and asserting the theme of history repeating itself. Judge Mettrick refers to two similar instances from the past when a town collapsed under the strain of external threat: Athens in the fifth century B.C. and nearby Indian Falls—eight years earlier.

Yet the most cursory analysis reveals the allegorical quality of *High Noon*, that Hadleyville in the 1870s is representative of American society in 1952. Foreman and his collaborators are not so much teaching history as using it to illustrate a point: that the political machinations known as "McCarthyism" could destroy the fiber of American society the same way Mitchell and his gang were about to destroy Hadleyville. Seen in this perspective, *High Noon* is a clarion call rallying individuals to stand up for what is right in the face of adversity, and it is reassuring in its message that a single courageous person can make a difference. That theme of personal responsibility was expressed again, for exactly opposite political reasons, by Elia Kazan in *On the Waterfront* (1954). Kazan's rebuttal was in turn answered by Martin Ritt in *Edge of the City* (1956) and in Arthur Miller's plays "The Crucible" (1954), "A View from the Bridge" (1956), and "After the Fall" (1956). The political "dialogue" in which these various writers and directors engaged is alien to today's students, and it would be valuable to screen Woody Allen's *The Front* (1977) to acquaint them with Hollywood during the Cold War and the McCarthy era.

A sociologist could discuss *High Noon* as a microcosm to evaluate how a community responds to external threats, or he could frame the town's reaction in the context of the early fifties, comparing and contrasting it with how American society coped with the twin menaces of Communism and the zeal of those who would do anything to crush that ideology. He can deal with the microcosm through the theories of Whitney H. Gordon in *Community in Stress* (1964) and Richard Harris in *Fear of Crime* (1974). The literature on the McCarthy era is enormous, but the arguments are well summarized by Paul Rogin in *The Intellectuals and McCarthy: The Radical Specter* (1967), especially those of sociologists Daniel Bell and Seymour Martin Lipsett.

Other sociological elements of both a historical and an immediate nature are the role of women, the treatment of minorities, and the place of religion in community life. In all three circumstances, information and messages are conveyed forcefully, though it is not always clear if the historical or contemporary context is under scrutiny. The role of women as subservient to men is aggressively stated by Helen Ramierez—"He's your man!"—though her entire life in Hadleyville has been one of independence and self-sufficience as a saloon proprietor. Prim and proper Amy Kane describes herself to Helen as "strange": "I am a feminist. You know women's rights—things like that. . . ." There is a conflict between the words and actions of each woman that reflects human complexity. Conversely, Mrs. Fuller is described as "a simple woman" who does her husband's bidding; and the women who speak out in the church meeting are ignored.

Helen also laments being both a woman and Mexican "in a town like this. . . ." Indians are a faceless minority as they plod about, speaking no lines. Blacks are totally absent, as they are in virtually all westerns, though recent studies have proved that there was a significant number of black cowboys in the West. Religion is painted as a formal exercise for respectable citizens: Marshal Kane is reminded that he does not come to church very often, and the minister criticizes him for being married in a civil ceremony. The town religious leader is cast in a less than flattering light. After saying that "The right and wrong seem pretty clear here," he declines to lead his congregation: "I don't know what to say . . . I'm sorry." The message is plain that religious leadership is as ineffectual as its political counterpart when strained, and that individual convictions falter when seriously challenged. That latter observation is equally true when applied to Amy, but her deviation is presented as praiseworthy rather than deplorable. The only other time that religion enters into *High Noon* is in its identification of Amy as a Quaker, adhering to the stereotype that the sum total of Quakerism is an abhorrence of violence.

Psychologists will find in *High Noon* several descriptions of human motivation, which is as much a tribute to John W. Cunningham's analyses in his short story as to the filmmaker's adaptation. Appreciating and understanding why people react as they do and what prompts their behavior can be accomplished by examining each character individually. The dialogue is particularly direct, and viewers are left with little uncertainty. One might charge the writer with oversimplification in all of his characterizations except that of Will Kane, but he is trying to characterize larger classes within each individual. Harvey Pell is motivated by jealousy within a guilty conscience, and Amy is compelled by religious beliefs that she ultimately abandons. Both are victims of their pride, as is Helen Ramierez and Kane himself. Foreman's "personal" nemesis, Sam Fuller, is a coward motivated by fear, a common trait of townsmen who try to mask their anxiety behind economic and other tangential explanations.

Will Kane's psyche is deeply probed: there is responsibility—"I'm the one who sent him up"; a blind sense of duty—"I've got to, that's the whole thing"; male ego—"They're making me run. I've never run from anybody before"; and fear—"This is crazy. I haven't even got any guns." Critics of *High Noon* who perceive it as an allegory for the McCarthy era stress the first two motivating factors, but careful viewing and reading of the screenplay will reveal the importance of the last two. Indeed, the allegorical quality is partially undermined by that emphasis within the narrative. Courage emerges as an emotional—but not irrational—response to the force of events. Because he understands the community better than Kane, Judge Mettrick, in his decision to flee, displays more common sense. Psychologists can assess the behavior of each individual, calling upon an endless literature that includes David Birch's *Motivation: A Study of Human Action* (1966) and Charles Cofer's *Motivation and Emotion* (1972).

The historical aspects of *High Noon* will be of less value to psychologists than they are to historians, political scientists, and sociologists. Even social psychologists will be inclined to evaluate the ideas as reflective of the human condition generally rather than at some specific point in time. In a similar way, few westerns will be of great use in unraveling the web of human emotions. Westerns, like other action-adventure productions, play down the multitude and complexity of factors that prompt particular behavior patterns. Explanations tend to be simplistic and obvious, and there is a preference for the amorphous "our's is not to reason why, our's is but to do or die" when coping with carnage. Screen versions of the defense of the Alamo, from George Nicholls, Jr.'s *Man of Conquest* (1939) to Frank Lloyd's *The Last Command* (1955) to John Wayne's *The Alamo* (1960), are indicative of that predilection. Exceptions to this rule are Henry King's *The Gunfighter* (1950), Delmer Daves' *3:10 to Yuma* (1957), and Michael Winner's *The Lawman* (1970), the last two of which draw much of their inspiration from *High Noon*.

Psychologists intent on examining the variety and complexity of human behavior patterns and what motivates them would probably be better served by avoiding westerns, even "psychological" westerns, and turning to the work of Orson Welles, Otto Preminger, Alfred Hitchcock, and other directors noted for their ability to analyze the human psyche. Other efforts of Stanley Kramer, for example, *Inherit the Wind* (1960) and *Judgment at Nuremberg* (1961), are also valuable source materials.

Philosophy students will realize that ethical considerations are intertwined with psychological ones in the scheme of Kramer, Foreman, and Zinnemann. Each character is confronted with an ethical-moral choice in determining how he will participate both as an individual and as part of a group during a community crisis. The film is probably weakest when it evaluates ethical dilemmas—the minister did say that "The right and wrong seem pretty clear here." The filmmakers were so intent on conveying their message of only Will Kane and Amy making the proper ethical decision that they engaged in overkill. In that way *High Noon* is typical of the western genre. Westerns have always handled ethics and morals in a simplified, straightforward way. Their enduring popularity can be attributed in part to the reassurance that audiences receive from portrayals that are morally and ethically clear-cut. Struggling in a society in which ethical dilemmas and moral confusion are commonplace—situation ethics being the norm—the images of people confronting unambiguous choices is reassuring for viewers.

The ethical question bothering the reviewer for *Catholic World*, "Is a man conscience-bound to fight for the right when those he would save repudiate him?" is answered at the end with a purported clarity; but the purpose is exactly the opposite. The final scene, in which Will Kane grinds his marshal's badge in the dust, is a hammer blow that stuns rather than enlightens. Because of it, many viewers must completely reevaluate their initial impressions. Grinding the badge irritated John Wayne and his friends in the Motion Picture Alliance for the Preservation of American Ideals, who first misunderstood the intent of the filmmakers and saw the picture as a tribute to law and order.

SOME ADDITIONAL REQUIREMENTS

As noted above, classroom use of *High Noon* by any discipline presumes that students are familiar with the history of America at the height of the Cold War and the role that Hollywood played during the McCarthy era. I would not make that assumption, however, and I would advise lecturing on the subject or assigning readings. I. F. Stone's *The Haunted Fifties* (1963) is a good start. Similarly, since *High Noon* is a prototype of the post-World War II "adult" western, some film history is imperative. Both of these exercises should be done with virtually any movie.

Finally, *High Noon* represents an opportunity to educate students about the fundamentals of filmmaking. Students think of a movie as a seamless web and rarely appreciate that it is the result of a deliberate constructive process in which many people have played a part. Ideally, before taking a film course in the liberal arts, students should be exposed to "Film Appreciation." Because most will not have had that experience and consequently have problems with visual literacy, the teacher will have to acquaint them with some of the basics. *High Noon* is an excellent movie for that purpose. Shooting in black and white with some interesting camera angles and lighting, very elaborate editing that won an Academy Award, and a musical score that is integral to the pace and creation of dramatic tension are among the features that can be identified and discussed.

EPILOGUE

I have proposed the documentarian methodology because of its facility for adoption by the novice and because of its expansive capacity for the competent, not because of some innate superiority to any other. That it places demands of varying degrees upon the students, demands that the teacher can control, is equally important. The use of movies in the classroom should be introduced slowly so that the student audience is not overwhelmed. Beginning with one or two features of the entertainment caliber of *High Noon*, with its potential for elementary or profound interpretation, will assist in developing a forward momentum.

The lines of approach delineated above are artificial, drawn as examples. No discipline has an exclusive domain, and the overlapping of subject areas in an interdisciplinary way will enrich the complexity of the entire film experience. Multifaceted productions are desirable because of the flexibility they offer the teacher. One-dimensional films lead to quick dead-ends. What can one say about a Busby Berkeley "Gold Digger" production after stating the self-evident, that 1930s audiences went to movies to escape the horrors of the Depression? Much of the ire of Stuart Samuels and others is directed at monolithic methodologies focusing on monolithic films. The supple characteristics of the documentarian approach mesh nicely with elastic conceptualization, film selection, and execution.

FOUR | INTERMINGLING PRACTICALITY WITH PEDAGOGY

ONCE HAVING determined to proceed with movies in the classroom, teachers must deal with a number of practical, technical, and pedagogical considerations that are intertwined. This interrelationship is important to recognize because these are not just a collection of so many minor annoyances. Selecting a topic, establishing goals, and formulating a methodology that fits your conceptualization are the most fundamental decisions to be made; but whether the goals are realized hinges greatly on how well the instructor succeeds in dealing with a wide range of details. The entire process of filmic instruction can be likened to a mosaic, in which the alteration or adjustment of any of the interdependent parts immediately affects all others; and like a mosaic, the final result is a product of conceptualization *and* execution. The best plans will falter or prosper according to the ability of the teacher to carry out each stage of the process.

I emphasize the importance of the execution or administrative phase of film-media instruction because it is so alien to the professional experience of most academics. At best, teachers may have a passing familiarity with the intricacies of film equipment if they have had collegiate training in it, usually in education departments. That instruction, however, is likely to be narrow and thin, normally leaving out a wide range of technical and practical matters during a brief survey of the entire world of audio-visual instruction. Most teachers have been educated almost exclusively in the world of print, and the technical aspects of the celluloid world can be frightening, perhaps crippling. Those who have occasionally brought a film into the classroom have found that they could do that by leaning heavily on others with more expertise. That kind of reliance or dependency is not possible in more elaborate situations.

Understanding the significant distinctions between print-based instruction and the movies is an important fundamental for appreciating many of the technical ramifications. Except that it is also an instructional vehicle, a movie bears very little resemblance to a book. A movie is an immediate, lifelike experience that envelops the viewers. Relatively speaking, watching a movie is a rapid occurrence that does not permit pondering an idea before others are presented. (Viewing on commercial television, with its periodic messages from sponsors, theoretically allows the spectator time for thought, but the normal responses to commercials are to watch them, to converse, or to leave the room for some reason. Many attribute the apparent increase of talking in theaters to a generation of viewers accustomed to watching television in the privacy of their homes, where they converse regularly during the telecast and the commercials.) Few productions run in excess of two hours, and the nonstop quality of a movie gives the appearance of a seamless fabric not always apparent in a book, especially if the latter is organized into chapters. But movies made exclusively for television have shown a tendency to be segmented into units or scenes like book chapters or play acts, organized to meet the demands of commercial interruptions. The verisimilitude inherent in movies, enhanced by such factors as costuming and casting for likeness, also lends a degree of realness and credibility that the medium does not always deserve.

Repeating the total experience is difficult if not impossible, and extracting salient excerpts is a cumbersome task. Video cassettes and video discs will ultimately make it easier to repeat the process, but I am dubious that opportunities for repeated viewings will benefit students. The simple reason is the expenditure of time. Going over one's notes from a lecture or a reading takes only a few minutes; re-viewing a two-hour movie always takes two hours. Furthermore, if they know that the film can be watched again, many students will not pay careful attention the first time. This is the same situation that has emerged from using audio recorders to tape lectures. I find most students only half listening while they are taping, figuring that they will heed what is said more carefully while playing the tapes back in privacy. But they very quickly amass hours of tape; they are overwhelmed by their collection and end up doing poorly in the course.

Print-based teaching is in many ways virtually the opposite: the instructor and/or reader can determine the pace of the process; a book or an article can be approached as a whole or in parts; pondering before continuing and re-reading what is not clear are simple activities; repeating the experience—especially in an age of photoduplication—is always possible, as is singling out certain ingredients for special attention. One could include numerous other examples of how film and print teaching are different and how practical and technical elements are responsible for many of those variables. A step-by-step description of the procedural aspects will reveal most.

BUDGET

David Sohn has correctly observed that budgeting problems have undermined much of the interest that faculties have in using movies in their courses. That film instruction in all forms came into prominence in the 1960s cannot be separated from the fact that that decade was an exceedingly affluent one. The flush times of an expanding economy and the grants of large sums of money, especially by the federal government, prompted experimentation with teaching approaches previously ignored because of prohibitive costs. Unfortunately, that financial largess waned in the 1970s, just when the flow of innovative techniques began trickling down to the mass of teachers. Declining enrollments, inflationary price increases, and a "Proposition 13" mentality have made "austerity" and "retrenchment" bywords in the educational world. Facing more demands than they have resources, department chairpersons, principals, and deans are reluctant to subsidize high-cost operations, particularly ones whose academic validity they are suspicious of.

The stringent economic facts of life dovetail into another traditional problem in the liberal arts. Regardless of the availability of funds, administrators are unfamiliar with requests for financial support from social scientists and humanists. It is assumed that the sciences require substantial economic aid because proper instruction calls for laboratories and supplies; but historians, sociologists, and the like have always survived with simple classrooms and chalkboards. Psychologists have made some progress in obtaining funds by becoming more scientific, and economists have succeeded in convincing administrators that today's student must be skilled in the use of the computer, so financial support has been provided.

Most of us, however, have been our own worst enemies. We have not educated our superiors in what our needs are. Even "advanced" thinkers in the administrative realm believe that a few slide and movie projectors and a modest sum to purchase some slides and rent a documentary or two are more than adequate. We have perpetuated the misconception that reading, lecturing, and discussion are all that are necessary for teaching in the liberal arts. The only resource beyond the classroom has been the library, and centuries of persuasion have led to the presumption that the size of the library—its number of volumes—determines the quality of an institution. Having spent millions to construct and maintain libraries, administrators gasp at the thought of spending even more for repositories of visual materials or using limited resources to rent films. We are paying a stiff price today for libraries whose principal function is to accommodate students who want a quiet place on campus to study.

The three factors of dwindling finances, a belief that a chalkboard is all that is required for classroom teaching, and the assumption that a well-stocked library is the only support service essential to the liberal arts combine to make obtaining funds for movie-based instruction a formidable task. Add to that a suspicion or hostility based on a feeling that showing movies is academic prostitution, and the dilemma looms even larger. Consequently, wisdom dictates that before requesting funds one must fully acquaint the administration with his goals and purposes. Converting colleagues is mandatory, for their support or opposition can be pivotal. A campaign well in advance of a funding application is the ideal way of proceeding, and any solicitation should be accompanied by a complete description of the project, couched in the most persuasive terms. A thorough and articulate explanation of the proposal, grounded in pedagogical terms, is essential; the teacher must convince administrators that his goals are worthwhile and can only be reached via the movies.

But all of us have had or are familiar with instances when the best proposals were rejected for any number of reasons. Experience has shown that the most convincing argument is one that focuses on cost-per-student estimates. While the total outlay of several hundred dollars may shock administrators initially, breaking the figure down according to how much will be spent per student will ease the blow. Such a presentation assumes that movie-based instruction will be attractive to an exceptionally large number of students, which is likely. (Promotional advertising among the student body is highly recommended at first. Even Hollywood has learned that its products can sometimes be made to succeed by advertising, and multimillion-dollar budgets are now allocated for that purpose. It used to be that advertising was only used to "save" a foundering picture, which is accomplished today by its sale to television.) The liberal arts disciplines have been experiencing the greatest decline in enrollments, and administrators are disposed to listen to propositions in which a teacher will appeal to and instruct a theater full of students instead of a relative handful. That kind of mathematics is very attractive and will be more convincing to protectors of the budget and department chairpersons than the most brilliant pedagogical design. One well-executed film course can favorably alter an entire department's faculty-student ratio, saving positions and permitting others to offer the esoteric courses that are thought essential for a well-rounded program.

The size of one's budget depends on several variables. Generally speaking, one can expect a semester-length offering, in which one movie per week or two is shown, to cost between $500 and $1000. The average film rental will be approximately $75. Depending on the subject and how flexible one is in picking movies, it is possible to do something for less than $500. For example, topics relating to World War II, the West, and crime can be negotiated for smaller sums because of the large number of productions available at low cost, some for as little as $25. On the other hand, one can spend thousands for recent releases, which tend to rent in the $250 to $500 bracket. That is the price range for the student-directed, entertainment-focused operations that are on virtually every campus. Another possibility is buying video cassettes and discs that are appearing on the market in the $40-$100 range. I have some serious reservations about showing movies on television sets in the classroom, a subject I will discuss in more detail later. From my vantage, I am more optimistic that video cassettes and discs of movies will lead to a reduction in rental fees from 16-mm film distributors. That likelihood, however, may drive some smaller distributors out of business and have the negative impact of reducing the number of features available. The trend in the distribution business already is toward oligopoly, with its attendant problems.

Certain generalizations can be made about movie rentals, because suppliers are competitive businesses responsive to market situations. In that context it is important to remember that classroom users compete with other non-theater renters, such as student groups who obtain features for purely entertainment reasons and charge admission. Most distributors provide movies for the classroom at a fixed rate for a single showing where no admission is charged and will scale down that rate for subsequent screenings. Other renters pay a predetermined fee plus a percentage of admission revenues, as the teacher will if he charges his students. Distributors are being somewhat generous in maintaining a dual price structure, though their generosity is prompted by a desire to maximize rentals of prints they in turn have leased from studios. The base rental will be computed according to whether the film has commercial possibilities, that is, if people will pay admission. The greater the commercial rental potential, the higher the base rate will be. Usually, the more recent the production, the larger the cost will be, and vice versa. That standard, however, will not hold true in the case of older films that for some reason have acquired a fashionable popularity, as have those starring Humphrey Bogart. Yet what is popular can also change. An obvious illustration are movies about the American Revolution, which were in heavy demand during the Bicentennial; rates for them in 1976 were much greater than in 1975, and they have since returned to earlier levels. How many agents have a print and how many prints a single operator has influence the rental structure also.

Some distributors, aware of the realities of the academic world, will on occasion significantly reduce the fee for a high-priced picture that is not in great demand at the moment, if one makes a courteous request. That is especially true for regular customers. Similarly, some will lower the per-picture cost if several are rented at one time for a single semester. Others will make no adjustments. When in doubt as to whether a distributor will be accommodating to one's circumstances, it is best to phone and discuss the situation rather than to write a letter.

Rental expenses are also dictated by other factors. Some companies have a minimum charge regardless of other considerations. One has a base rate of $40 and another of $75. I have found that there tends to be a direct relationship between the size of the distributor and its rates, and I have frequently found the same film renting from a smaller outlet at a much lower price. While the absolute minimum rental is $20 or $25, few productions, except those less than five years of age, cost more than $100. Movies of recent vintage, which command large sums, usually do so for only a relatively short period. Once a picture has appeared on television and made the rounds of student groups, the price will drop rapidly. Inflation, however, is taking its toll in the rental business too, and these figures will have to be modified periodically.

The teacher should familiarize himself with as many distributors as possible (a list is provided in the appendix). Most teachers are aware of the more prominent distributors of documentaries and instructional films since they are ordinarily media centers in universities like Syracuse and Penn State. Companies that rent Hollywood features rarely if ever handle documentaries or instructional productions. Most of them provide catalogs free of charge, and one should get as many as possible. Be careful of catalog descriptions; they are advertising "hype," particularly when they tout classroom suitability. When choosing between distributors, one should not make price the only consideration. The quality of the print—clarity of the sound track, number of splices, fidelity of color, location of reel breaks, and so on—and the dependability of prompt delivery are crucial elements. There is no easy way to assess these variables, although normally the larger the firm, the more reliable it is likely to be. Often, spending the extra money can be a worthwhile investment.

Some movies cannot be obtained from more than one source, because certain distributors have exclusive rights or others do not believe particular features have a market potential and drop them from their catalog listings. Even more are not available at any cost. The number of features that can be rented are a sizable minority of what has been produced, and it is not uncommon to learn that the "perfect" picture cannot be located. When that happens, academics, accustomed to prodding librarians into purchasing special books, should inform distributors of their preferences. Because of the relative newness of teaching with movies, suppliers are not as familiar as they might be with market possibilities. Also, because companies do not always list everything they have in their catalogs, an inquiry may return a positive response. Catalogs are issued yearly as a rule and contain only those items the distributor has reason to believe will be profitable.

A recent innovation that may grow is the practice of an institution's leasing a movie over an extended period, usually a year, for infinite usage at a cost of anywhere from $500 to $1000. Except for video cassettes and discs, it is impossible to purchase prints of feature films as one can buy documentary or instructional pictures; nor can one legally show a rental more than once without extra charges. More importantly, because all movies are copyrighted, one cannot exhibit any feature and charge an admission without paying a fee directly or indirectly to the copyright owner. (It used to be legal to tape virtually anything except movies off television because so little was copyrighted. However, because Vanderbilt University was videotaping the nightly network news and then renting their tapes, CBS sued to enjoin that practice, and almost everything on television is now copyrighted.)

I have already indicated my own reluctance to become involved in leasing arrangements. They will either commit the teacher to repeated showings, which he may not want, or force him into a compromising situation with other teachers to share its use. The latter means negotiating to find something that appeals to all, and that will require securing inter- and intra-departmental cooperation in advance. Not many administrators will lease a picture for $1000 simply to say that it is available for anyone interested. Yet, potential for combined use does exist, and leasing may mature into a common practice.

Once the teacher has pursued all of the angles and determined his budget, other means for financing exist if administrative funding fails to materialize. I would stress, however, that administrative funding is the easiest way of operating. Other mechanisms are less certain and have more problems; they should only be considered as second choices.

The most typical alternative and one that appeals to administrators is charging a fee comparable to the traditional laboratory fees in the sciences. The amount of the charge could be a set sum each semester, possibly large enough to build up a surplus that could offset fluctuations in enrollment. Another way is to vary the figure according to anticipated enrollment and the estimated budgetary needs. Both of those formats are hazardous because the course might not attract sufficient numbers, and someone will have to make up the loss. Also, potential enrollment can be adversely affected by a fee, with the size of the class reduction directly related to the cost involved. One could compromise with the administration by using income from the students to defray only a portion of the total expense.

The student fee technique raises a complicated legal problem. What seems a nominal and inconsequential fee to cover the expenses of an academic enterprise, not to make a profit, may be an admission charge to a distributor. Some will adjust the rate, demanding a share of the revenues, and the fee scheme becomes counterproductive. Some will accept such an arrangement as legitimate, and the number is increasing. Before setting a fee and signing a rental contract for which one's institution is liable if it is breached, one should learn the attitude of the distributor. I have known schools that have charged fees without forewarning distributors, as I have known those who pirate movies by videotaping from telecasts. Both actions are illegal. Never attempt to cheat a supplier. Most of them employ spies who visit institutions secretly to learn if the terms of the contract are being fully met. Rental receipts are so great today that copyright owners have even resorted to hiring people to count the gate at local theaters to prevent fraud.

Another way some instructors have obtained funding

is by cooperating with student organizations, often the most financially solvent groups on campus. Student assistance can be obtained in two ways. One is for the instructor to have a student group rent a film he wants at a time he needs it and admit his class. That method has proved successful at many schools. It is a great way to obtain expensive movies of recent vintage whose costs are beyond the academic budget capacity under any circumstances. The major drawback is that while a few films can be negotiated this way, it is difficult to build an entire course around a student film series. Also, most student-sponsored exhibitions are in the evening, and some students who have signed up for a 10:00 a.m. class may be reluctant to go. A second way of acquiring student aid is for the instructor to convince students to rent his film and to show it during his class, whenever it meets. The compromise would be to open that screening to members of the sponsoring group or to the student body at large. Doing that, however, opens up the legal question of whether or not the showing is within the contract provision of classroom usage. The distributor should be consulted; he may assign a different rental rate.

If all else fails, the teacher can fall back on television and local theaters, both those that exhibit first-run features and those that show retrospectives. In some ways, relying on television and local theaters is an act of desperation, and an integrated course could never be assembled around what may happen to appear. Yet they are valuable resources for complementing classroom activities. Keeping informed as far in advance as possible, an instructor can call student attention to pictures that can contribute to the understanding of a subject with which he has already familiarized them. Not all will cooperate, but those who do will find their academic experience enriched in their living room or neighborhood movie house. If a teacher strongly recommends or requires that students see a film outside of class, he should by all means comment on it afterwards and possibly discuss it if enough have seen it. By providing insights about contemporary productions, one can heighten student acceptance of the relevance of the approach and help bridge the gap between the classroom and real life; equally important, he will promote improvement in their visual literacy.

Overall, the best way to get money is via a direct administrative grant. Moreover, procuring such a grant is a testimonial to administrative support and faith in the project. Other measures have possibilities, at least as adjuncts if not entirely self-sustaining, and one may be able to build a unit around a few films financed by others. Regardless of which mechanism or combination is used, the size of the budget will play a role in how well a teacher accomplishes his goals. As suggested earlier, certain topics, because of the number of films addressing them, permit a latitude of choice that other, more circumscribed subjects do not. Less than adequate funding may lead to compromises, such as reducing the number of movies shown or selecting substitute pictures appropriate to the subject but not quite as strong as the original selections were. How far one can go in the spirit of compromise is limited by pedagogical expectations; one may prefer cancellation to compromise. If reducing the number of films or altering choices begins to undermine the ultimate purposes of showing movies, the validity of the technique disintegrates.

SCHEDULING

Probably the most underrated phase of movie-based instruction is class scheduling. Most college professors and high school teachers are used to thinking and planning in 40- to 60-minute units. Unfortunately, feature films take an average of 90 to 120 minutes. The longtime head of Columbia Pictures, Harry Cohn, insisted that none of his company's productions exceed two hours. He believed that that was the extent of the public's ability to sit in confined circumstances. Not all studios agree with that axiom, and many movies, especially classics like *Gone With the Wind* (1939) and other historical epics like *Ben Hur* (1959), run to three hours or more. Since television, some producers think that more celluloid is necessary to convince audiences to pay inflated admission prices at a time when the double feature has become a thing of the past.

Scheduling represents a quandary whose full implications are not always immediately recognized. In addition to the obvious practical problem, several questions of good teaching come into play. How students will intellectually digest a movie and how an instructor will realize his intentions are substantially determined by the format in which the movies are watched.

One innovation of recent years is the introduction of productions that have been edited to accommodate ordinary class periods. One might call this the *Reader's Digest* approach to movie-based instruction. The concept dates from the American Historical Association Feature Film Project of 1969. Recognizing the instructional dilemma of scheduling films, the AHA engaged several experts to supervise the editing of six historical pictures, including *Juarez* (1939) and *Martin Luther* (1956). The distributor, Films Inc., has sponsored a similar series called The American Challenge Film Program, which offers *The Grapes of Wrath* (1940) and *Wilson* (1943), among others. This company has also organized The American Film Genre Program, a series of productions suitable for courses in film appreciation.

A comparable venture is the fifteen-film program Searching for Values, A Film Anthology, dating from 1972. The films are 15- to 20-minute extracts assembled by the Learning Corporation of America and designed to provide students with a values-clarification experience in several disciplines. *Whether To Tell the Truth,* scenes culled from *On the Waterfront* (1954), probes the theme of conscience and conflicting loyalties; *Politics, Power and the Public Good,* scenes taken from *All the King's Men* (1940), examines the issues of abuse of power and whether ends justify means. These programs actually are instructional films, since students are expected to learn from them, not analyze them.

While these edited renditions have the virtue of neatly fitting time allocations, opinion varies about their academic validity. The debate focuses on the issue of whether using abbreviated pictures, films shortened by someone other than the director, is recreating an experience comparable to that of the entire movie. Opponents contend that external editing is artificial tampering, that the messages and information as organized and developed by the director are hopelessly lost by the reduction. Critics emphasize that the students should have the same experience as original audiences; to reduce two hours to thirty or forty minutes is so radical, it is believed, that something new is created in the process. The debate is reminiscent of the controversy over the final cut of Bernardo Bertolucci's 1900 (1978). The director fought efforts of his producer and distributor to shorten his mammoth production, and film critics throughout the world rallied to the opposing sides.

Others endorse the reduction procedure, noting that it is commonly if not as extensively done for television, a prime source of student familiarity with movies. (Editing for television is steadfastly opposed by some directors, notably Otto Preminger, and others insist as part of the sale contract that they must supervise the editing. Only recently have viewers been forewarned with the leader "Edited for Television" that what they are seeing is something less than what was shown in the theaters.) Moreover, supporters contend that the significant elements have been maintained in the editing and what was excluded is not necessary for achieving their goals. Regardless of one's viewpoint, only a handful of movies are available in abbreviated format, and the AHA has ended its program in the face of cost and criticism. It remains to be seen if the commercial endeavors will be continued and expanded.

Because most teachers will use feature films in their entirety, the essential question is how best to do that. The ideal way is to screen the movies in a single sitting as in theater exhibitions. One showing minimizes problems with absent students who may miss portions with extended screening, and it lessens memory lapses and failure to appreciate the uniform flow of the film. On the other hand, some students may not see the movie at all if it is only shown once. One-day viewings also avoid difficulties with distributors who rent their wares with that in mind. Most distributors will cooperate if one's schedule dictates viewing over several days, but that kind of usage should be discussed in advance to prevent late return penalties.

At the college level single screenings frequently can be scheduled for late afternoon or evening, if administrators are cooperative. The same might be true in high schools, though it is more difficult to arrange. Administrators can be persuaded to alter normal scheduling patterns for the liberal arts if one draws a comparison with the elongated time slots set aside for scientific laboratory classes. Teachers can promote student willingness to go out of their way to meet the demands of one-time viewing by increasing the credit allocation from the usual three to four. Again, one can convert hesitant administrators by drawing an analogy with the extra credit assigned to courses with laboratories. Otherwise, enrollment may suffer because of the feeling that additional labor is not being rewarded. My experience has shown that evening screenings are especially popular in residential institutions, where students integrate going to the movies with normal social patterns. The late afternoon is a better time for commuter facilities and high schools because of a reluctance to return to campus after dinner.

While I highly recommend the one-showing procedure, I also feel that nothing else should be scheduled for that period but watching the movie. A few introductory remarks are in order, and the teacher may wish to entertain a few questions, especially of a content nature, because sometimes students will miss something. Critical film viewing requires a considerable expenditure of physical and mental energy, and to try to do more than watch will strain student patience and intellectual resources. Lecturing before and/or discussing the film afterwards will extend the class period to intolerable lengths. More importantly, the quality of discussion will deteriorate. The most crucial phase is the discussion, and it will languish and be minimally productive, if not counterproductive, if it is held immediately after viewing. I say this with the full realization that many movie-based college courses meet only weekly, and that lecturing, viewing, and discussing are all done at one time. I strongly question the academic integrity of that technique. It is very popular with students, but it is pedagogically unsound.

Screening over an extended period is a second choice, but a valid one. A teacher can minimize what is lost by requiring attendance and promoting continuity. One can help with the continuity by determining that the breaks arrive at the most desirable times, not just the end of reels. Distributors have an annoying habit of putting as much film on a reel as possible, and the breaks can be very dislocating. Try to limit the duration as much as possible, perhaps three days at most and preferably consecutive days. Students should be alerted that extended viewing will demand more of their critical viewing skills; and the instructor may have to jog their memory by introducing each segment with a commentary on what has transpired.

No matter what approach is followed, screening a movie is a three-staged process: tell the viewers what they will see, show the movie, and then tell the viewers what they saw. That description is crude but apt. Students have serious deficiencies in visual literacy, and many teachers will discover that they have a similar handicap. The state of visual literacy is virtually identical to its print counterpart. Studies of the results of the Scholastic Aptitude Tests have proved that most students after reading something can recite the narrative, but few can analyze or interpret. The same is true for the visual media. Just because someone can watch, a seemingly effortless activity when compared to reading, does not mean that they understand what they see. As I recommended earlier, one can look at the students while they are watching, and many will have that same glassy look in their eyes that they have at home in front of the television. Visions are going into their brain, but whether they are having an impact is questionable.

Movie-based instruction is an analytical and interpretive experience that calls for more than a recapitulation of the plot. Before turning down the lights, the teacher should prepare the audience with preliminary insights about the plot structure and some interpretive dimensions. Risks that the students will miss some of the information and messages will be smaller if they have had classes in the rhetoric of film or film appreciation, where they learn how to watch a movie. (Such a course might be considered as a prerequisite, and enrollment can be increased by negotiating trade-offs.) Students have a habit of turning off their brains when the light switch clicks, and the teacher must emphasize the importance of keeping their minds active and alert. They have to learn to be active participants rather than passive recipients.

Postviewing discussions should begin with an overview of the principal information and ideas before moving on to more intricate analysis. Students have an inclination to focus on minor elements, minutiae and trivia, at the expense of perceiving the larger scene. The "can't see the forest for the trees" syndrome is common. They will come up with a definition of reality or authenticity taught them by filmmakers. In Hollywood, accuracy is having the details correct. Consequently, students will count the number of bullets fired in a western, note the correctness of uniforms and armaments in war pictures, and observe car models, hairstyles, and clothing fashions in more contemporary movies—while failing to notice deeper aspects. I once showed Raoul Walsh's *They Died With Their Boots On* (1944), a cinematic rendering of the Custer massacre, as a way of examining Indian-white relations. When I began the discussion by asking if there were any questions, the first student wanted to know if they had cold beer in the West. His mind had been riveted on an inconsequential bar scene, and he spent the remainder of the screening wondering about irrelevancies while missing the whole point of the movie. I am reluctant to criticize students too much for this failing because accuracy of detail is what they have been led to believe is important. What we have to do is to teach them that there are many more significant facets that must be assessed.

Pre- and postscreening obligations, as well as other pedagogical demands for thorough coverage of the topic, can be handled in normal class periods scheduled at any time of the day. College instructors can arrange other functions around a standard Monday-Wednesday-Friday or Tuesday-Thursday schedule so long as the film is sandwiched between preparation and analysis. The same holds true for the Monday through Friday sequence of high schools. Because viewing is more convenient in the late afternoon or evening, that does not mean that other classes must be at the same time. Nor must the procedure be fully negotiated within a week. More than one class meeting can be devoted to preparation or to discussion. How much time is given to lecturing, discussion, and readings will depend on the capabilities of the students and how long it takes the teacher to prepare them for viewing and to conduct an intelligent post-mortem.

MOVIE SELECTION

Several variables influence decisions on what features are to be used: budget, what is in the rental market, whether a print is available on a certain day, and, most importantly, the instructor's knowledge of what films are useful. Composing a course that includes all of the films that the instructor thinks essential hinges on these elements, and orchestrating them is a challenge. Along with these practical considerations is another with significant pedagogical implications—student attitudes about what constitutes a good or entertaining movie. It matters little if the teacher has obtained the cheapest rental rate and stayed within budget while getting what he wanted if the movie bores the students. Remember, what the teacher thinks is a great or entertaining film is not always the opinion of the audience. I have found it very enlightening to ask the students at the end of the semester to rank the films according to their opinion of the entertainment quality. I am not saying that the primary concern should be entertaining students. Rather, I am stating that the instructor will be more successful if the students find the viewing experience enjoyable.

The teacher's familiarity with the primary source materials is imperative for the best possible selection. Becoming acquainted with a film through the print medium is useful and valuable, especially for what one can learn from other specialists in the field who may have reviewed the production from an academic vantage point. *Film and History* regularly contains reviews, and other professional journals should be encouraged to follow suit. Periodical and newspaper reviews tend to be most valuable for information about the narrative, factors during production, and occasionally something about audience reaction.

When selecting a film, the teacher should take into account how recently he saw it and whether it was from the perspective of classroom utility. Memories are faulty, and what is recalled fondly may or may not be suitable. Movies do not age well: technology is always changing, and the art and technique of filmmaking evolves. Thus films are easily dated, a dimension that can be an asset or a liability. Unfortunately, today's student demands a technically superior product; he considers watching television or a movie in black and white a sign of cultural deprivation. He expects films to be in color, wide-screen extravaganzas complete with stereophonic sound, popular stars, casts of thousands, elaborate costumes, intricate special effects, and so on. The subject matter must be exciting and calculated to appeal to current tastes. Students, the financial mainstay of Hollywood, are used to being wooed by producers competing for box-office success. Unfamiliar titles breed apprehension, and as a general rule the newer the film, the more popular it will be. Professors J. Joseph Huthmacher and James J. Curtis of the University of Delaware have conducted an extremely popular course entitled "The American Dream on Film." Their success stems partly from using many relatively recent productions that were originally aimed at youthful audiences, for example, *The Graduate* (1968), *Downhill Racer* (1969), and *Little Big Man* (1970), sprinkled with well-known classics such as *Birth of a Nation* (1915) and *The Grapes of Wrath* (1940). I hesitate to estimate what their budget might be, but their approach packs the students in.

Students also have little toleration for the older, slower-paced films designed for the less visually attuned public of the thirties and forties. Titles of Humphrey Bogart, James Cagney, and Edward G. Robinson gangster movies will appeal to them because those are currently chic, but one can watch their attention wander as the picture slowly unwinds. They have difficulty identifying with actors they do not recognize, and vicarious identification is undoubtedly the most critical factor in determining entertainment value. With rare exceptions, students despise silent movies, an attitude that can be partially changed by engaging a piano player. Silent-era audiences expected and received musical accompaniment; why should today's student be different? Some distributors, especially the Museum of Modern Art, provide sheet music for a few of their silent rentals, and good players, then as now, can improvise. The uniqueness of this experience usually generates enthusiasm.

Student preferences can be altered somewhat if they have a background in film appreciation and if the instructor is candid in acknowledging at the outset that not all of his choices will be considered entertaining. A good strategy is always to start the course with a movie that is high on the students' scale of entertainment and then alternate the more and less "entertaining" ones. Of course, when academic needs clash with student opinion, the teacher's decision must be paramount. Some film history and appreciation will help counter hostility to having to watch "dull" movies. Also, teachers should not be misled by the reactions of their first class. One's initial offering is likely to draw a skewed audience, including every buff on campus. These individuals with a better than average understanding of the movies may not only be more tolerant of older features, they may be eager to watch them. Their replacements in later semesters will be more representative, and it is this latter group with which the teacher will have to deal most often.

Finally, to paraphrase P. T. Barnum, do not overestimate student sophistication in spite of their protestations. Polling audiences over several years in a topical approach to American history has revealed that action-adventure movies, almost regardless of age, are considered the most entertaining and hence the most popular. Movie courses about World War II or the West have been my highest enrolled, most satisfied classes.

ORDERING

Ordering is a distasteful, time-consuming clerical task. From checking the inventory to find out what is available at what price to mailing the print back to the distributor, one can expend a considerable amount of time and energy. Because renting a movie is an institutional requisition, precise methods will vary. If media specialists or librarians are available, use their expertise, because it can prevent tragic blunders. They may be helpful in the selection process, but be cautious of leaning on them too heavily. One of their standard complaints is that they and not the teachers wind up doing the creative work of selecting and booking films. They are most useful for coordinating the business end of things, an element with which most academics have only minimal competence.

The cardinal rule of ordering is to do so at the earliest possible time, preferably several months in advance. Prints are limited, competition is great, and distributors have no objection to early booking. This rule holds true for documentaries and other kinds of films also. Movies are not like books, where a late order can be rush delivered. Last-minute phone orders can be done with motion pictures if a print is available, but that is a risky proposition. Further, the impossibility of renting one particular movie may cause the change of other orders that are already confirmed. Ample time should be provided for adjustments. At the other end, cancellation is possible, generally up to two weeks before the scheduled showing, though the exact time varies according to distributor. Booking a film does not require a deposit, so a teacher can order what he wants for when he wants it without fear of losing anything.

Time expenditure, duplication of effort, and ulcer-producing anxiety can be avoided by phoning distributors before sending written requisitions. Most will accept collect calls, and for those who do not, the modest expense is worthwhile. Written follow-up is required, and distributors will forward contract forms. These contracts specify date, time, place, approximate audience size, and price of admission if any. Because of variable rate structures, specify that it will be used for academic purposes. Schools are eligible for credit accounts, a practice that simplifies payment. On receipt of contracts, distributors will return copies and written notice of confirmation.

Written confirmation of a rental is not a guarantee that the print will arrive on time. Prints are returned late, suppliers sometimes book too closely, clerks err, and the U.S. Postal Service and private carriers are not always punctual. If the film has not arrived forty-eight hours before it is scheduled to play, the instructor should call the distributor. That allows the distributor time to rush another print if he has one or to negotiate a substitute if possible. Distributors will understand one's concern and will try to cooperate. The greatest danger—especially on the college level where rescheduling is often impossible—is for a print to arrive late or not at all.

Immediate return of a print is a mandatory provision of all rental agreements; delay will lead to additional charges. Postage and insurance are either paid by the renter, or sometimes they are included in the handling fee. By all means, the print should be insured for its approximate value, at least $500, because the teacher is responsible for its return. One should calculate approximately ten dollars per picture as part of the budget for this expense.

Damaged prints, anything more than a broken splice, will result in further expense. Most distributors prefer that a print be returned without rewinding; they do that themselves on a machine that inspects the print while rewinding. Improperly wound films, too tight or too loose, are the most common cause of jammed projectors and print breaks. Distributors promise to provide materials in perfect condition, which is naturally not always true. During prescreening, one should note any damage for future reference and have it repaired if possible. Students will be distracted by uncorrected situations such as print breaks; they grow restive enough with simple reel changes.

Do not alter the print in any way. Many people have cut scenes for inclusion in their private library. I once rented *Knute Rockne—All American* (1940), only to discover that the immortal "Win one for the Gipper" scene had been cut out. Complaining to the distributor, I learned that it had been done for legal reasons. I was then lectured about the growing incidence of prints that had been snipped.

EXHIBITION

Screening a movie is more involved than turning down the lights and switching on the projector. The frequently mentioned predicament of poor visual literacy becomes apparent during viewing, but one can do several things to improve the quality of the experience and to maximize student comprehension.

The need for thorough preparation of the students has already been stressed numerous times. That procedure includes a comprehensive indoctrination in the purposes and methods of the unit. Those things, of course, can be done with any combination of lectures, readings, and discussions before the film is shown. Wisdom suggests that students be so versed in the subject matter prior to screening that all would not be lost if a print failed to materialize or if a student was absent.

Beyond providing the factual standard of reference necessary for analyzing the movie, the most difficult problem the teacher will encounter is that of deficiency in critical viewing skills. The woeful state of visual literacy is in large measure the result of the ingrained habit of turning off the brain simultaneously with the lights; the presumption is that viewing is such a simple process that anyone can do it without exerting any intellectual effort. Deeply implanted habits must be destroyed and others created. A good way to start is by convincing students that viewing is a mind-expanding educational experience. They must be persuaded that the same degree of seriousness and intensity given to reading or following a lecture should be applied to watching a movie. Taking notes should be encouraged, if not required.

Teachers can stimulate visual literacy as well as improve students' understanding of the film's relationship to the subject by distributing a series of thought-provoking questions to be answered in writing *before* any discussion. Another mechanism for accomplishing these tasks is to have them maintain a diary of their observations. Structured according to the teacher's directives, the diary forces students to think and to commit their ideas to paper. The teacher should read these diaries periodically and offer constructive criticisms. Diaries have the advantage of permitting each student to move along at his own pace. Depending on how serious the problem of visual literacy is in his class, the instructor might consider making reference books available. Among the better ones are: John Harrington's *The Rhetoric of Film* (1973), G. Howard Poteet's *The Compleat Guide to Film Study* (1971), and *Understanding the Film* (1976) by Ron Johnson and Jan Bone. The last is designed specifically for high school students. Also available for rent are films on how to watch films, though these are not especially well done.

The dilemma of poor visual literacy that I have emphasized so strongly is something that is finally being recognized and accepted by educators generally. For years, most were either unaware of the problem or refused to acknowledge it, preferring instead to assail movies and television as purveyors of mindless aberrations. It was a situation of wanting to kill the messenger because they did not like the messages. Realizing that television and the movies are here to stay (it has become impossible to ignore the fact that a high school graduate has spent 12,000 hours in school and 17,000 hours watching television) and that pseudo-intellectual posturing against the "idiot box" has had no effect, the Department of Health, Education, and Welfare decided to fund a program entitled "Critical Television Viewing Skills."* Several education centers around the country are developing print materials for distribution to teachers in primary and secondary schools. That it is being done without any visuals is ironic, but the program is a welcome step in the right direction. The skills that are to be transmitted will have comparable application to the movies and should significantly reduce visual literacy problems in movie-based instruction.

I try to convince my students that during the exhibition they should keep a mental distance between themselves and the rest of the audience and the movie itself. That can be done by imagining that they are not actually sitting in the theater but are in the lobby watching through a window. What happens is that they become an observer rather than a viewer. Intellectual detachment is important, for if they become a part of the audience, the likelihood is that they will be swept away by the captivating nature of the visual presentation. Directors want that; they want people to become engrossed in what they are communicating, and most people readily succumb. I ask my students to fight the tendency to slide back in their seats and let the movie become their world as long as the lights are out. Were it possible, I would have my students do their viewing with the lights on. The darkened theater is a world all its own.

---

*Regrettably, the first federal grant for improving viewing skills was the recipient of Senator William Proxmire's "Golden Fleece Award."

I also attempt to persuade my students to be independent agents when viewing. That is, I encourage them to avoid becoming part of the larger group, the audience, and responding to the visual stimuli as others do. For most students, going to the movies has traditionally been a group social activity, and they are inclined to react to what they see as others around them do. It is a simple case of peer pressure, because even in the darkness friends and strangers alike can see how one responds. That is why most people who go to pornographic movies do so alone; they don't want anyone to know how they are reacting. What a teacher needs to do with students is to get them to conceive of watching a movie as a personal experience separate from a group activity.

All of these things can be done, though it will usually take the better part of a semester before the students are conditioned to critical viewing. With luck it will become a habit that they carry over into their daily lives. I have had many students "complain" that they can no longer enjoy a movie as they once did, that they find themselves critically assessing it rather than turning their brain off. That is the greatest compliment one can receive.

DISCUSSION

The last stage, discussion, is the most important. The three-pronged evolution of preparation, viewing, and follow-up is such that the last aspect is what makes the first two meaningful. It is during the discussion that everything comes together and a whole is created from the several parts.

As I have mentioned, immediate postviewing discussion should be limited and voluntary. Most students will feel that they have done their part by viewing as directed, and if they have done it critically their minds will be tired. However, the process of critically viewing and note-taking while being exposed to a rapidly moving picture can cause some confusion, and there may be some specific questions about the content of the narrative. Any misunderstanding should be clarified as soon as possible. But ample time should be provided for contemplation, to allow students' minds to digest and assimilate what they have seen before launching an analysis.

Depending on how and why the film has been used, the discussion will revolve around the reinforcing, comparative, or contrasting qualities of the messages and information. The form of the discussion can be predetermined by the written questions the students have answered; the audience will thus know in advance where the discussion will begin, and they will be prepared. The instructor should read the answers as he would their diaries, commenting on their observations in such a way as to encourage more productive veins and to discourage digressions. If he does not read them—possibly even grade them—students will not take the exercise seriously. As it is, they rely heavily on talking among themselves before committing their thoughts to paper. The teacher will have to monitor them closely so as to be certain they are writing individual opinions and not the product of a group effort.

Examinations and written assignments can function as well in movie-based instruction as in other formats, and they will influence the quality of the discussion. Because they contribute to the grade, students are careful to attend and participate in the discussions. Well-constructed essay examinations are good learning experiences, but objective questioning is dangerous because it tends to reaffirm predispositions toward trivia and detail unless the questions are very imaginatively designed. More likely to succeed, both for purposes of completing the educational experience and for developing a basis for grades, is requiring papers. I recommend a series of short papers instead of a single long one. Experience has shown that the quality improves substantially with each paper, partly because the first attempt is usually disastrous. The teacher should select the topics —individual or uniform—and the design can be research oriented or it can emphasize collating, in an original way, information, insights, and perspectives that have emerged from the universal components of the course. The comparative or contrast method lends itself more to papers than examinations. Requiring brief or extended reviews, drafted as a professional in that field would draft them, can serve as a preliminary to more detailed assignments. Some teachers stop with reviews, but I would not recommend that. Teachers should provide outlines for how they are to be done; otherwise students will follow the practice of most newspaper and periodical reviews and summarize the plot.

Whichever techniques or combinations are used, one should be very careful to avoid erring in the extremes of too little or too much. Students already assume that movie-based instruction is easier than other approaches, and too few demands will sustain that belief and fortify the suspicions of hostile colleagues. But there is also a danger in overcompensating, of assigning more reading and writing than one ordinarily would in order to protect himself from criticism and to prove that standards are being upheld. Too much will discourage students and result in declining future enrollments. Assigning a number of small, repetitive tasks of increasing difficulty that culminate in a few major papers and/or an examination is desirable, but the cumulative result should be equivalent to the demands of any other instructional technique.

FIVE | UTILITARIAN CONSIDERATIONS AND RESEARCH POSSIBILITIES

THE INTERACTION of instructional requirements and utilitarian concerns is an ongoing process in movie-based instruction, and a continuing awareness of the smallest details of their relationship will facilitate that interplay. The following discussion is designed to point out the most practical and technical facets of the process, an understanding of which will ease the multitude of classroom responsibilities. Opportunities for going beyond the classroom and into personal research projects will also be discussed. The teacher's involvement in investigations of immediate interest to him will unquestionably improve classroom performance, and student response to lecture materials that incorporate little-known information and insight is often superb.

VIEWING SITUATION

The location for screening a movie is a significant consideration that is often overlooked. The standard classroom, with desks or armchairs neatly organized in straight rows, is a poor facility for watching a movie. Sight lines are bad, acoustics are generally not very good, and effective darkening of the room is difficult. The last can be a nuisance when there are many windows with shades instead of heavy drapes; viewing can be nearly impossible because of the eyestrain. However, because of the importance of note-taking, some type of soft, recessed lighting, carefully balanced in brilliance between the needs of watching and writing, is preferable to absolute darkness. Moreover, asking students to remain attentive while confined in less than comfortable desks for two hours or more is asking too much. Handicapped by limited attention spans already, students are further distracted by the discomforts of hard, uncushioned seats and straight, unpadded backs.

Most colleges and high schools have auditoriums or theaters, and these should be used whenever possible. Such facilities may be absolutely necessary for an exceptionally large class. But even if one's group only occupies the first few rows, try to arrange for a theatrical setting. The picture will invariably be larger because of the screen size and projector lens, and tiering will improve sight lines. Central sound reproduction systems and an auditorium designed with a concern for acoustics will make listening easier. Portable projectors, like portable television sets, have notoriously poor speakers. Most school theaters also have projection booths, which means that the sound of the running machine will not interrupt viewing. Lighting can ordinarily be adjusted too. Seating is comfortable, though writing may be awkward if writing arms are unavailable. In addition, auditoriums or theaters have a psychological value. Familiarity with the setting stimulates a positive student attitude toward viewing, although one must be careful to prevent that attitude from degenerating into a casualness that impairs visual perceptiveness.

Conducting lectures and discussion in such an expansive area may or may not be desirable according to the individual teacher's technique, enrollment, and goals. Discussion is especially difficult with large enrollments, and I advise breaking the class down into smaller, more manageable units. That makes it easier to work with the students and enhances the learning experience. But both arranging for a proper viewing facility and forming discussion sections from a larger class can cause scheduling difficulties that should be settled in advance. On the university level, graduate assistants can serve as discussion leaders. Team teaching is another way of providing sufficient staff to direct small group discussions as well as to bring divergent perspectives to the same material. Working with a colleague has the added benefit of sharing clerical duties.

The foregoing assumes the use of 16-mm film and a projector. If the teacher shows—that is, telecasts—the movies on videotape or discs, the situation will be much different. In that case a theater environment will not be desirable because of the difficulty of seeing monitors no larger than twenty-five inches at a distance of more than ten to fifteen feet. The teacher will most likely prefer a series of smaller, more intimate rooms.

I would strongly recommend that, if it is necessary to use videotape or discs, it be done with video beam systems that have five to seven feet diagonal pictures rather than standard receivers. My reason for that recommendation is grounded in the way students respond to watching large screens as opposed to small ones. There is something about the larger-than-life quality of the images on a theater screen, even the portable models, that compels people to focus their attention, and most do. Dark or semidark theaters also reduce the likelihood of visual distractions. While they are not obeyed as closely as they once were, social conventions dictate that theater viewing be done in silence and with a minimum of movement.

Watching small-screen television receivers is a different activity that elicits a different response. Their presence is not as commanding; the environment is casual. Accustomed to television viewing in the totally unrestricted confines of their homes, students are not used to watching carefully. They may give the impression of watching intently because of the glassy look in their eyes, but habitual mesmerization should not be confused with cognitive assimilation of what they see. Talking and roaming around is generally done during programming and always during commercials. Those habits intrude into the classroom, especially if it is difficult to see the monitor. The common practice in schools of placing receivers high on side walls at ten-to fifteen-foot intervals is terrible. They may be easier to see than if they were in front of the room, but looking up and over will cause the neck to stiffen in a matter of minutes. The lighted room fortifies an impression of informality that students already have about watching television. Furthermore, while they may be attuned to viewing with very small groups such as their family, watching in a crowd of twenty, thirty, or more is strange, and they do not know how to act.

Another matter of consideration is the psychological viewing pattern of most students. While they all conceive of both the movies and television as entertainment media, that predilection is stronger with television than the movies. Students will concede that movies can be, perhaps even should be, occasionally thought-provoking as they entertain. They are willing to accept the idea that producers, writers, and directors may be trying to communicate ideas that are worth noting. Television, on the other hand, is exclusively entertainment for them. When one turns on a television set, they will expect to be entertained, not educated, and it will be difficult to persuade them differently. Educational television is thought of as a contradiction in terms, and to use their favorite source of entertainment to teach them is greeted as a prostitution of sorts. By the time students have reached high school, they will have long since soured on the idea anyone can or would want to learn anything from television. Most reviewers agree that commercial programming that has the imprimatur of the National Education Association or similar organizations almost always is a victim in the ratings. Students will also expect that the telecast be interrupted every ten to fifteen minutes, as is done commercially, and their attention span is geared accordingly.

It is for these reasons that I earlier argued against using videotapes or discs of movies rather than 16-mm projectors. If video cassettes must be used, I recommend the large-screen video beam systems. They are an improvement because they simulate normal movie projection, and they do generate student responses comparable to those in other large-screen situations. Although video beam systems constitute an acceptable compromise, they are not without their problems. As with all television receivers, picture definition and color clarity suffer when expanded. The units are costly, retailing for around $1500 for videotape and half that for disc systems, and the apparatus is sensitive in the hands of the untrained. Continuing technological changes may alter these conditions in the near future, but I advise caution in the meantime.

If a teacher does become involved with videotape and purchasing video cassettes of movies, there are two other factors to keep in mind. The first is that there are two types available, V.H.S. and Beta. They are not compatible. Those in the industry speculate that the demands of the home market will lead to the extinction of one, though neither has yet to demonstrate an obvious superiority to the other. No one is sure which one will take over, and the school could wind up with some expensive obsolete equipment. The same circumstance holds for incompatible disc systems. The second consideration concerns how much equipment will be needed. Because the teacher will be buying, renting, or borrowing cassettes, the school's tendency is to purchase only playback machines in order to minimize expenses. For the additional cost, small relative to the initial outlay, I suggest the purchase of a recorder also. In an institutional setting a taping capacity will have infinite uses. Because of the problems with pirating, it is also conceivable that copyright owners may one day allow taping of movies from telecasts for a modest fee. Unfortunately, the cheaper disc operations are exclusively playback machines and do not have a recording company.

THE MYSTERIES OF THE 16-MM PROJECTOR

Very few faculty members have more than a rudimentary knowledge of movie projectors. Mechanical breakdowns, such as the malfunction of the automatic threading apparatus, leave them helpless. The vast majority of teachers rely on others for equipment purchases and have had little or no input into decisions that are affected by rapidly changing technology. While the result, the picture or the image, appears substantially the same regardless of what kind of projector is obtained, several variables between brands exist which may make a particular machine more or less desirable.

Showing a movie requires a projector and screen. With the exception of size, there is no real difference between screen types, and any will suffice. The only exceptions to that generalization are three-dimensional projection, Cinerama, and what is generically known as Cinemascope, although that is a brand name. One can only view 3-D, another patented process, with a special beaded screen and Polaroid glasses. Cinerama requires three separate curvilinear screens and three interlocking projectors. The few films available in either 3-D or Cinerama and the equipment demands fairly well preclude academic use. Twentieth Century-Fox's Cinemascope and its competitors simulate three-dimensional viewing and call for a 146° curved screen, the approximate range of human vision. Cinemascope has a picture with a 2.55:1 or 2.35:1 width-to-height ratio, whereas "flat" projection has a 4:3 ratio. The projector requires an anamorphic lens to spread the picture. It is increasingly possible to rent Cinemascope copies, usually at the same price as a flat print, and students will be very impressed with it. The difficulty will be to convince one's school to buy the larger screen and to purchase 35-mm or 70-mm projectors, since that is the usual size of Cinemascope prints. Some distributors have introduced 16-mm cinemascope prints, but the number of films remains small.

The essential piece of equipment is the portable projector, designed during World War II for the military to show movies in the field, and the standard film size is 16-mm. A few productions are available in 8-mm or Super 8 (they are not compatible), but those have generally been superseded by video cassettes and discs.

Probably the most common 16-mm projector for institutional use is the Bell and Howell Autoload, a tribute as much to the corporation's marketing department as to the virtues of the machine. Kodak provides a competitive model, though it is not self-threading, and dozens of others are now on the market. All are manufactured to accept a variety of lenses from one to four inches in diameter, depending on focal length and size of picture desired. A one-inch lens will project a maximum of twenty-one feet. The larger the picture—96'x72' is the maximum—the poorer the definition will be, but in all cases it will be superior to its televised counterpart.

Of those currently available, the most versatile and simplest to operate is the Singer Graflex. This projector functions much like an audiotape recorder, with a capacity for fast forward and fast reverse. No other machine can change speeds during projection. A footage meter helps define particular segments, and one can easily cut to a specific scene or repeat one as often as is desired. It is also the best machine that I have seen for stopping on a single frame; and a half-projected reel can be removed, something that cannot be done with any other model. Though not an automatic-threading projector, the loading procedure is actually easier than those that are supposedly automatic. It is virtually impossible to jam, and the loops do not slip as readily as they do on other models. It is wise to get the best projector available because of the number of different people who will use or abuse it in an institution, and because many prints are worn and thus prone to causing mechanical problems.

One feature to look for in any projector is a capacity to change frame speeds. The standard speed is twenty-four frames per second, but silent movies were filmed at eighteen frames per second. The "jumpy" distortion of silent movies, which amuses or irritates students, is caused by increasing their frame speed by one-third. Unfortunately, no portable projector is equipped for slow motion, and most will burn the film when stopped on a single frame.

Even if the teacher uses a theater setting, and the projector is a permanent fixture, he will most likely be using what is nominally called a portable machine. A recent innovation, which has been slow to spread because of cost, is a 16-mm rear screen projector. This is a machine that is stationed behind a translucent screen and projects the picture through a series of mirrors. It does not improve the picture quality and has no particular virtue so far as I can tell. There is, of course, no light beam from the rear of the room, an asset for some but a liability for those who use that little bit of light to help students in their note-taking.

No 16-mm projector has a decent sound system. Like television, their emphasis has been on reproducing the picture, while sound has been a secondary affair. Projector speakers are small and have poor tone quality. All but the Kodak model have the speakers built into the projector, which means that those close by either hear well or are deafened so that those at the outer edges can hear. The Kodak machine has a detachable speaker that can be moved to a central location. The ideal is to be able to plug into a central sound system. Sound track damage is second to print breaks as the most common problem with rentals, and the normal wear of repeated use takes a higher toll on the sound track than it does on the picture.

Because projector breakdown can cause a cancellation and rescheduling headaches, the teacher should always thoroughly examine the machine before each screening. Most problems can be anticipated. Dust particles in sensitive locations are the most common cause of mechanical failures, and they can also damage prints by scratching them. Spare projector and sound bulbs should always be on hand, since those offer no warning before burning out, and extra fuses should also be nearby. If one has a familiarity with the working parts, a projector is actually a very simple machine, and there is no need to be afraid of it. Many times any teacher will be able to make a quick, temporary repair if he has studied the machine.

A second projector is a valuable asset. Besides insuring against the disaster of mechanical failure, another machine prevents time loss while changing reels, a five-minute project if all goes well. More importantly, twin projectors (all movie houses have two) provide for a smooth flow between reels and enhance the continuous quality that a movie should have. Students become restless during reel changes because of the disruption of their concentration. A full reel has a running time of approximately forty-five minutes, more than ample time to make a discrete change while the students are watching the screen.

Of course, nearly all of these problems can be minimized or avoided by having a skilled projectionist other than the instructor. They are less likely to accidentally damage a machine or a print, and they are better prepared to make repairs. Furthermore, a projectionist frees the instructor to attend exclusively to classroom matters. Besides watching students to determine their responses, the instructor may also find it necessary to wake them up or discourage disruptive activities. An absolutely dark room may encourage some to catch up on their sleep, especially if they have seen the movie before. That is another reason for soft lighting. Students should be supervised during a screening just as during any other classroom activity.

LOCATING AND DISTRIBUTING READING MATERIALS

Uncovering print sources that bear a one-to-one relationship to a particular film can be difficult. The secondary literature is substantial, always expanding, and improving in quality. Publishers have responded to a growing readership of educated people by shifting much of their emphasis away from the coffee table pictorials toward books with more substance. These studies will be useful for the teacher's preparation, but it is not always practical to assign them to students. They tend to include much extraneous information, and requiring one book per film will overburden the class. An anthology like *American History/*

American Film, with its fourteen selections, is perfect if one happens to be showing the same movies. Teachers will want to build their own courses around their own selections, not those of someone else. But even if just some of the selections coincide with those in *American History/American Films,* this book could be a valuable asset.

Journal articles remain the best secondary source. *The Journal of Popular Film and Television,* an exceedingly diverse collection in spite of its title, is a quarterly that is indispensable. Other professional journals, especially those in American Studies such as *American Quarterly,* regularly publish articles on film, and even staid traditionalists are becoming more receptive. The decision of the *Journal of American History* to issue an article in its June 1977 issue about the movies, "What to Show the World: The Office of War Information and Hollywood, 1942-1945" by C. R. Koppes and G. D. Black, was a milestone. However, until the academically oriented secondary literature becomes more extensive and inclusive, one will have to rely heavily on primary sources such as newspaper and magazine articles for support.

Although finding materials that deal directly with a specific film can be difficult—many movies are over-studied while others are ignored—locating sources relative to the picture's content, its place in film history, and the historical epoch surrounding its premier is far easier. Every teacher has the research and library skills necessary for discovering information about the content or subject if its basis is in fact, which most movies are. If the production is entirely fictionalized, the task of finding readings that parallel and reflect on the subject matter is a simple matter. Locating a motion picture's place in film history is not difficult because of the many general histories of film available. The number and range of film histories is so extensive that the most obscure movies are at least mentioned. As for acquainting one's students with the historical milieu in which the movie appeared, there are so many histories of every facet of twentieth-century America that I am reluctant to begin enumerating them. As European historians frequently say about the study of American history: "Never has so much been written about so little."

Because it is usually impossible to uncover the perfect source, except by assigning an entire book devoted to the film one is teaching or possibly arranging the course around an anthology, I have found that the easiest thing to do is to collect a series of readings and make them available to the students. These readings may vary from a page or two, such as a review, to as much as a chapter from a book. These can be placed on assigned reading in the library or given directly to the students. In either case, photoduplicating is the solution to the problem of retyping lengthy extracts. Making individual photocopies, of course, can be expensive, and it may be necessary to put only a few on reserve in the library. It is best for every student to have his own copy, and that can be done with a Xerox Thermofax copier. That machine will take a single Xerox photocopy and make a master that can be used on a fluid duplicator. The cost reduction is enormous.

I have known some instructors who have compiled a packet of photoduplicated reading materials and sold them to the students to recover the costs. Some inflate the charge in order to cover film rentals too. They justify or legitimate the approach by drawing a comparison with traditional laboratory fees that schools levy to offset the cost of supplies.

Regardless of the means of duplication, recent changes in the copyright laws dictate extreme caution. The legislation is extremely ambiguous, and one should examine it closely before proceeding. It may be necessary to obtain permission of the copyright owner and pay a fee. That is certain to be the case if one intends to sell duplications.

MOVIES AND RESEARCH FACILITIES

Becoming conversant with the more than 30,000 American movies that have been produced, of which approximately 10,000 prints survive, of which a few thousand can be rented, is tedious. The place to begin is to request as many catalogs from commercial distributors as possible. Their sales personnel do not visit schools as do those of book publishers. But once one is on their mailing list, most will keep their customers up to date on any changes. Not all distributors will automatically send a new catalog each year, and one should always reorder, if for no other reason than to keep current with price changes. The catalogs generally include Motion Picture Association of America ratings, and major awards the film has won, but they do not indicate for what level of maturity or intelligence the particular movie is suitable. Catalogs of documentaries and instructional productions ordinarily provide evaluations, noting that a particular film is suitable for adults only, or adults and high school students, or junior and senior high school students, and so on. The M.P.A.A. classification system has been in operation only since 1968, or 1966 depending on one's definition, but the standards or determinants have steadily changed. Without the necessary knowledge and caution, one could accidentally book for an immature audience a movie that has nudity or vulgar language. Useful adjuncts to distributor catalogs are: Ernest Limbacher's *Feature Films in 8mm and 16mm* (rev. ed., 1971), Artel and Kathleen Weaver's *Film Programmer's Guide to 16mm Rentals* (1972), and specialized works such as *The Guide to Films (16mm) About Famous People* (1969), which enumerates 1,450 titles about 1,180 "famous" individuals, and Paul Spehr's *The Civil War in Motion Pictures* (1961).

Two paperback references that are absolutely essential are Leslie Halliwell's *The Filmgoer's Companion* (6th ed., 1977) and Leonard Maltin's *TV Movies* (rev. ed., 1978). Halliwell provides an international encyclopedia with over 6,000 entries. The overwhelming majority are names of individuals, but he also discusses several hundred topics, fictional characters, and terms. He incorporates a few film titles, generally classics, and describes those productions in some detail. Maltin offers an alphabetical listing of over 12,000 movies that have appeared on television, including the 800 made-for-television features produced since 1967.

Each title is accompanied by the copyright date, the running time, a one-to-four star rating of the entertainment value, names of the director and principal actors, and a brief synopsis, often opinionated. Stephen Scheuer's *Movies on TV* (1978) is comparable, and a teacher should own either Maltin or Scheuer if for no other reason than that they identify those productions with which students are most familiar.

Other reference works are valuable, but none compares with *The American Film Institute's Catalog of Motion Pictures Produced in the United States, Feature Films 1921-1930* (1970) and its companion for the 1960s. Each is a two-volume study with an organizational scheme comparable to but more detailed than Maltin's. The research for the twenties was monumental, with full descriptions of hundreds of silent productions whose prints have been lost to antiquity. This was to have been a decade-by-decade series up to the present, but it has been suspended for lack of funds.

The United States does not have a central repository for movies. Federal legislation mandates that two copies of any copyrighted material be deposited with the Library of Congress, and such a library could have been established. However, storage difficulties, accentuated by the highly volatile nature of the early nitrate stock, discouraged the ostablishmont of ouch a facility. Thc major studios have preserved their prints in fireproof vaults, and some stars maintained collections of their pictures, but countless studio and independent productions have been irretrievably lost because nitrate stock is subject to decomposition and disintegration as well as fire.

The Library of Congress finally created a Motion Picture Division of its Paper Print Collection in 1939, and it has selectively exercised its option to acquire movies since then. It has also made some effort to obtain pre-1939 productions, and the American Film Institute houses its extensive holdings at the Library. The AFI is a child of the motion picture industry and is supported jointly by public and private moneys. One of its important projects is preserving older nitrate movies by transferring them to celluloid. This process of restoration and preservation of prints obtained from many sources has greatly expanded what is at the Library of Congress, but it is far from exhaustive. To this day it continues its policy of selective acquisition, so the problem of missing movies will never end.

The Motion Picture Division is a public facility open to all qualified researchers, though the projection facilities are quite limited, and one must travel to Washington to take advantage of it, since prints are not dispensed on interlibrary loan. Similarly, distributors do not provide free previews of their feature rentals as they do with the documentaries they sell. Occasionally, they will be cooperative and allow a teacher to look at their wares if he is willing to come to their headquarters. As a result, it is difficult to develop a firsthand familiarity with movies other than by viewing them in theaters and watching television. Most film historians readily admit that they could not do their research without late-night television.

Other facilities that house motion pictures include the Academy of Motion Picture Arts and Sciences and the Walt Disney Archives in Hollywood, the Museum of Modern Art in New York City, and George Eastman House in Rochester, New York. A disastrous fire in 1978 destroyed a significant portion of the latter's collection. A few colleges maintain film archives, notably the University of Wisconsin, which holds all of the Warner Brothers features, and the collections at the University of Southern California and the University of California at Los Angeles are substantial. Since its demise, RKO Pictures has donated its complete production to the Wisconsin Historical Society. One can only hope that other studios will also make that decision or build their own research facilities as Fox-Movietone News did.

RESEARCH AND PUBLICATION

Teaching with movies will almost automatically lead to a desire to conduct some kind of research and perhaps to publish one's findings. As I noted earlier, the relative newness of movie-based instruction has led to the unfortunate circumstance that many persons are pursuing parallel tracks as each reinvents the wheel. Recognizing the redundancy, the needless repetition of mistakes, and the limited awareness of successes, many education journals, for example, *Media and Methods, Social Science,* and *The History Teacher,* welcome descriptions of creative classroom approaches. A few book publishers have accepted similar manuscripts, and Ralph J. Amelio's *Film in the Classroom* (1971) constitutes an in-depth analysis of three years of planning and revising and two years of teaching a high school film study program. The surface has been barely scratched, however, and I would encourage anyone who has something to offer to submit it for publication.

Whether or not a teacher writes for publication about his experiences, I would urge everyone to evaluate the results each time he uses movies in an instructional format. Every new approach should be assessed periodically, but the need is more pressing with film courses because of their complexity, their novelty, and their capacity for changes. The same structure and format will evolve differently each time, if for no other reason than the changes in the mix of students. Teachers also become more adept with each offering, modifying and adjusting as they go along. Any evaluation procedure should have considerable contributions from students, at least until movies become as ordinary in classrooms as textbooks. Reporting one's conclusions to the administration is likely to buttress their support as they come to better understand the value of movie-based instruction.

Many historians, sociologists, psychologists, and others in the liberal arts have shifted their traditional research orientation after they have taught with the movies. Exposure to the movies is intellectually infectious, and cinematists have had to learn to share the field. That sharing has led to an expansion of research approaches beyond the traditional approach to movies as artistic expressions. Because of the involvement of those in other disciplines of the liberal arts, we now find such diverse explorations as examinations of movies as reflections of popular culture and institutional analyses of studios by economists. Probably the most phenomenal growth has been in semiotics, or the study of the movies as a form of language or communication. The increasing willingness of editors to entertain manuscripts about the movies generally indicates that the 1980s should be a boom period for publication.

Doing research into the movies, regardless of disciplinary perspective, is arduous and time-consuming because source materials are limited and scattered. The failure of participants and observers to take the movies seriously in earlier years did not help matters when it came to preserving vital information. I have already noted the absence of a central film repository; the situation with print-media collections is not much better. The Film Study Department of the Museum of Modern Art is the best facility of its kind, but it is essentially composed of clippings and still photographs. The same is true of the Theater Research Collection of the New York City Public Library System, though it also contains some programs and exhibitor materials. The Archives of Popular Culture at Bowling Green State University maintains a modest inventory of print materials. The libraries of the Academy of Motion Picture Arts and Sciences, the University of Southern California, the University of California at Los Angeles, and Twentieth Century-Fox Studio, all in Los Angeles, represent the nearest thing to a centralized collection of printed sources.

Something substantial like the Museum of Modern Art's David Wark Griffith Papers, mainly correspondence, is rare. Lacking a historical consciousness, unaware that their work might have some value other than immediate financial rewards, most moviemakers either did not retain their files longer than required by the tax laws, or they directed that the files be destroyed after their death. Furthermore, the secretive nature of the film business did not prompt many filmmakers to maintain extensive collections of written materials. Those who did possess a sense of their own importance and that of their industry, and who kept their papers, usually did so with an eye for writing memoirs that would appeal to movie fans and the mass market. Given the notorious egocentricity of most filmmakers, they might very well be disposed to turn over what papers they have if archivists were to court them as they do politicians. Appealing to their vanity will have to suffice, because there is no longer any tax benefit involved. Until 1968 the Internal Revenue Code permitted deductions for the gift of one's papers, and politicians and other significant public figures were quick to donate their files. Since the change in tax laws, however, the number of private collections winding up in the public domain has diminished considerably, but that should not be a barrier to an aggressive solicitation of Hollywood moguls. Other persons involved in making movies, such as writers, editors, cameramen, and the like, should also be encouraged to make their materials public.

One solution to the dearth of written source materials is oral history, the process of interviewing participants and permanently recording their commentaries. Oral history is a technique that anyone can master. The historian Lawrence H. Suid has done so with astounding success. For *Guts and Glory, Great American War Movies* (1978), Suid interviewed over 300 individuals in all facets of the movie industry and government. By depositing his tapes at Georgetown University, Suid is laying the foundation for a unique collection with unlimited possibilities.

A dependence on interviewing to fathom the maze of Hollywood reflects the larger problem of how best to conduct research into the movies. As teaching methodologies are in their infancy, so too are their research counterparts. Research models are in short supply, and each scholar must determine his own techniques, establish his objectives, and develop individual approaches. Regrettably, duplication of effort, needless error, and unfortunate oversight are as much a part of the investigative process as they are of pedagogy. There is an urgent need for outlets for sharing research techniques. Journal editors and program directors for professional meetings should be as receptive to proposals for manuscripts and papers that elaborate on technique as they are proving to be to those that focus on content.

There is a very positive attitude on the part of public and private agencies to fund movie-based research investigations. The National Endowment for the Humanities, the American Council for Learned Societies, the American Philosophical Society, and the Rockefeller Foundation are just a few of the organizations willing to sponsor research projects. While the total allocation is modest compared to sums devoted to more traditional endeavors, it is noteworthy and encouraging that foundations other than those with a vested interest, like the American Film Institute, are stepping forward to assist.

The opportunities for researching the movies are virtually unlimited, and an imaginative observer will have no difficulty identifying suitable and worthwhile projects. However, teacher-researchers interested in exploring the intricacies of America's most popular art are advised to do so in conjunction with standard academic activities. Purists who are skeptical of film-based instruction maintain an equally suspicious attitude about film research. The untenured can jeopardize their future if they do not pay homage to the customs and conventions of academia. Furthermore, publishers have shown a greater interest in projects that bear a similarity to more traditional approaches. The likelihood of publication is increased if one integrates interdisciplinary considerations into a research methodology. Those circumstances will surely change in the near future in the same way that cynicism about movie-based instruction will wane. A few years from now we will look back and wonder why we were cautious or hesitant about teaching or researching the movies. But in the interim—until the fear of the new, the different, and the unknown fades, as it always has—I recommend the path of teaching ordinary classes in standard ways and researching and publishing in conventional veins in addition to one's involvement with the movies.

A FINAL WORD

This book is offered in the same spirit that prompted John Burnham to write *How To Teach History* (1970). After several years of directing and coordinating dozens of instructors and graduate students in an introductory survey at Ohio State University, Professor Burnham decided to recount his experiences and the lessons he learned so that others might profit from them. The outcome had very little to do with history. A more accurate and descriptive title of his work would be "How to Survive Your First Year of Teaching Without Making a Fool of Yourself or Being Fired." I highly recommend it for any novice, and even the most experienced teacher will find valuable insights.

The Burnham survival kit is a blend of the theoretical and practical in a forthright manner. His "warts and all" style may be grating and even offensive, but there is no mistaking his meaning. So candid is his expression, so revealing is he of the basic ingredients of pedagogy that are generally kept hidden, that Burnham was concerned that his volume might fall into the hands of the enemy—the students. Copies can be ordered only on letterhead stationery.

Accepting the accuracy of Stuart Samuels' prosaic description of film study in history courses—"a lot of bullshit" and "little careful attention"—and reacting to the opinion of David Weinberg (in an unpublished paper, "Methodological Problems in the Use of Film in the Teaching of Modern European History") that movie-based instruction has progressed far enough to withstand critical appraisal, I have attempted to convey my experiences and observations in a straightforward fashion. What I have written is not mere opinion but the product of years of involvement; I have expressed strong opinions on a variety of issues and have not tried to color reality. I do not mean to grate or offend, but the time has come, as Weinberg has argued, to bluntly discuss the use of movies in the classroom. Some of what I have written may seem at first glance to be self-evident to those with a background; but we who have developed that background have also been inbred and isolated, forgetful that the fundamentals are crucial for the uninitiated. My long-range goal is to promote serious introspection and stimulate a dialogue, to develop a dialectic process that will be ongoing and lead to the maturation of teaching techniques and research methodologies that will serve the needs of a visually oriented society.

SELECTED BIBLIOGRAPHY

The following compilation is not intended to be exhaustive, but is designed to identify basic works with which secondary school and college instructors should be familiar and which they might wish to include in their personal library. Those interested in more extensive sources should consult:

Bowles, Stephen E. *An Approach to Film Study: A Selected Booklist.* New York: Revisionist Press, 1974.

Bukalski, Peter J. *Film Research: A Critical Bibliography With Annotations and Essay.* Boston: G. K. Hall, 1972.

Dyment, Alan R. *The Literature of Film.* London: White Lion Publishers, 1975.

MacCann, Richard Dyer and Perry, Edward S. *The New Film Index: A Bibliography of Magazine Articles in English, 1930-1970.* New York: Dutton, 1975.

Monaco, James and Schenker, Susan. *Books About Film: A Bibliographical Checklist.* 3rd ed. New York: New York Zoetrope, 1976.

Rehrauer, George. *Cinema Booklist.* Metuchen, N.J.: The Scarecrow Press, 1972. See also *Cinema Booklist: Supplement One* (1974).

Nearly every volume devoted to film study published in recent years includes a bibliography slanted toward its particular focus. Furthermore, the number of books appearing annually on every facet of film is increasing at a dramatic pace, and it is as imperative to remain current as it is to be aware of what has been written in the past.

JOURNALS AND SPECIALIZED PERIODICALS

AITIA
American Cinematographer
American Film
Cineaste
Cinema
Cinema Journal*
Critic
Dialogue on Film*
Film
Film and History*
Film Comment
Film Culture
Film Heritage
Films in Review
Film Library Quarterly
Film Quarterly*
Focus on Film

The History Teacher*
Journal of Popular Culture*
Journal of Popular Film and
  Television*
Journal of the University Film
  Association*
Jump Cut
Literature/Film Quarterly*
Media and Methods*
Quarterly Review of Film Studies*
Sight and Sound
Sight Lines*
The Silent Picture
Studies in the Anthropology of
  Visual Communication*
Take One
Teaching Philosophy*
University Vision

*These are of particular value for teachers because they frequently publish articles from a pedagogical perspective.

REFERENCE WORKS

Esner, A. G. S. *Filmed Books and Plays: A List of Books and Plays From Which Films Have Been Made.* London: Andre Deutsch, 1971.

Gottesman, Ronald and Geduld, Harry. *Guidebook to Film: An Eleven-in-one Reference.* New York: Holt, Rinehart and Winston, 1972.

Halliwell, Leslie. *The Filmgoer's Companion.* 6th ed. New York: Hill and Wang, 1977.

Krafsur, Richard, ed. *American Film Institute Catalog: Feature Films, 1961-1970.* 2 vols. New York: R. R. Bowker, 1976.

Limbacher, James L., ed. *A Reference Guide to Audio-Visual Information.* New York: R. R. Bowker, 1972.

Maltin, Leonard. *TV Movies.* (rev. ed.) New York: New American Library, 1976.

Manchel, Frank. *Film Study: A Resource Guide.* Rutherford, N.J.: Farleigh Dickenson University Press, 1973.

Michael, Paul, ed. *The American Movies Reference Book: The Sound Era.* Englewood Cliffs, N.J.: Prentice Hall, 1969.

Munden, Kenneth, ed. *American Film Institute Catalog: Feature Films, 1921-1930.* 2 vols. New York: R. R. Bowker Co., 1976.

_____. *New York Times Film Review, 1913-1968.* 6 vols. New York: New York Times and Arno Press, 1968.

Samples, Gordon, *How to Locate Reviews of Plays and Films: A Bibliography of Criticism from the Beginnings to the Present.* Metuchen, N.J.: The Scarecrow Press, 1976.

Scheuer, S. S. *TV Movie Guide.* (rev. ed.) New York: Bantam Books, 1977.

VOLUMES DEVOTED TO FILM AND PEDAGOGY

Amelio, Ralph. *Film in the Classroom.* Cincinnati, Ohio: Standard, 1971.

_____. *The Filmic Movement: Teaching American Genre Film Through Abstracts.* Dayton, Ohio: Pflaum, 1975.

Coynik, David. *Film: Real to Reel.* (rev. ed.) Evanston, Ill.: McDougal, Littell and Co., 1976.

Culkin, John and Schillaci, Anthony, eds. *Film Delivers: Teaching Creatively With Film.* New York: Scholastic Bookservice, 1970.

Feyden, Sharon, ed. *Screen Experience: An Approach to Film.* Dayton, Ohio: Pflaum, 1969.

Gessner, Robert. *The Moving Image: A Guide to Cinematic Literacy.* New York: E. P. Dutton, 1968.

Harrington, John. *The Rhetoric of Film.* New York: Holt, Rinehart and Winston, 1973.

Hodgkison, Anthony W. *Screen Education.* New York: Cinesco, 1968.

Johnson, Ron and Bone, Jan. *Understanding the Film.* Skokie, Ill.: The National Textbook Co., 1976.

Katz, John, ed. *Perspective on the Study of Film.* Boston: Little, Brown, 1971.

Kuhns, William and Stanley, Robert. *Exploring the Film.* Dayton, Ohio: Pflaum, 1968.

Lacey, Richard. *Seeing With Feeling: Film in the Classroom.* Philadelphia: W. B. Saunders, 1972.

Mallery, David. *The School and the Art of Motion Pictures.* Boston: National Association of Independent Schools, 1966.

Maynard, Richard A. *The Celluloid Curriculum: How to Use Movies in the Classroom.* New York: Hayden, 1971.

O'Connor, John and Jackson, Martin. *Teaching History With Film.* Washington, D.C.: The American Historical Association, 1974.

Peters, J. L. M. *Teaching About Film.* New York: UNESCO, 1961.

Poteet, G. Howard, ed. *The Compleat Guide to Film Study.* Urbana, Ill.: National Council of Teachers of English, 1972.

Pronay, Nicholas, et al. *The Use of Film in History Teaching.* London: The Historical Association, 1972.

Sheridan, Marion C., et al. *The Motion Picture and the Study of English.* New York: Appleton-Century-Crofts, 1966.

Sohn, David, ed. *Good Looking: Film Studies, Short Films and Film-making.* Philadelphia: North American Publishing Co., 1976.

_____. *Film Study and English Teachers.* Bloomington: Indiana University Audio-Visual Center, 1968.

Stewart, David, ed. *Film Study in Higher Education.* Washington, D.C.: American Council on Education, 1966.

_____. *The Use of Film in the Teaching of English.* Toronto: The Ontario Institute for Studies in Education Curriculum, 1971.

GENERAL STUDIES

Armes, Roy. *Film and Reality, An Historical Survey.* Hammondsworth, England: Penguin Books, 1974.

Arnheim, Rudolph. *Film as Art.* Berkeley: University of California Press, 1957.

Ball, Robert H. *Shakespeare on Silent Film.* London: Allen and Unwin, 1968.

Barsam, Richard. *Nonfiction Film: A Critical History.* New York: E. P. Dutton, 1973.

Bergman, Andrew. *We're in the Money: Depression America and Its Films.* New York: Harper and Row, 1971.

Bluestone, George. *Novels into Film.* Baltimore: The Johns Hopkins University Press, 1957; Berkeley: University of California Press, 1961.

Braudy, Leo. *The World in a Frame: What We See in Films.* Garden City, N.Y.: Doubleday, 1976.

Cavell, Stanley. *The World Viewed: Reflections on the Ontology of Film.* New York: Viking Press, 1971.

Cripps, Thomas. *Slow Fade to Black: The Negro in American Films, 1900-1942.* New York: Oxford University Press, 1977.

de Heusch, Luc. *The Cinema and the Social Sciences: A Survey of*

Ethnographic and Sociological Films. Paris: UNESCO, 1962.

Eckert, Charles, ed. *Focus on Shakespearian Films.* Englewood Cliffs, N.J.: Prentice-Hall, 1972.

_____. *Film and the Historian.* London: British University Film Council, 1969.

Fenin, George and Everson, William. *The Western: From Silents to the Seventies.* New York: Penguin Books, 1973.

Fielding, Raymond, ed. *A Technological History of Motion Pictures and Television.* Berkeley: University of California Press, 1967.

Frair, Ralph and Natasha. *The Only Good Indian: The Hollywood Gospel.* New York: Drama Book Specialists, 1972.

Greenberg, Harvey R. *The Movies on Your Mind: Film Classics on the Couch From Fellini to Frankenstein.* New York: E. P. Dutton, 1975.

Haskell, Molly. *From Reverence to Rape: The Treatment of Women in the Movies.* New York: Holt, Rinehart and Winston, 1974.

Heider, Karl G. *Ethnographic Film.* Austin: University of Texas Press, 1976.

Higham, Charles and Greenberg, Joel. *The Celluloid Muse.* Chicago: Henry Regnery, 1969.

Huaco, George A. *The Sociology of Film Art.* New York: Basic Books, 1965.

Hughes, Robert. *Film: Book 2, Films of Peace and War.* New York: Grove Press, 1962.

Hull, David. *Film in the Third Reich: Art and Propaganda in Nazi Germany.* New York: Simon and Schuster, 1973.

Hurley, Neil P. *Toward a Film Humanism.* New York: Dell, 1975. (Originally published in 1970 as *Theology and Film.*)

Hurt, James, ed. *Focus on Film and Theater.* Englewood Cliffs, N.J.: Prentice Hall, 1974.

Jackson, Martin and O'Connor, John, eds. *American History/American Film.* New York: Ungar, 1979.

Jacobs, Lewis, ed. *The Documentary Tradition.* New York: Hopkinson and Blake, 1971.

_____. *The Movies as a Medium.* New York: Farrar, Straus & Giroux, 1970.

Jarvie, I. C. *Movies and Society.* New York: Basic Books, 1970.

Jowett, Garth. *Film: The Democratic Art.* Boston: Little, Brown, 1976.

Knight, Arthur. *The Liveliest Art.* New York: Macmillan, 1957.

Kracauer, Siegfried. *From Caligari to Hitler: A Psychological History of the German Film.* Princeton: Princeton University Press, 1957.

_____. *Theory of Film.* New York: Oxford University Press, 1970.

Lahue, Kalton C. *Continued Next Week: A History of Moving Picture Serials.* Norman: University of Oklahoma Press, 1964.

Leab, Daniel. *From Sambo to Superspade: The Black Experience in Motion Pictures.* Boston: Houghton Mifflin, 1976.

Limbacher, James, ed. *Film Music From Violins to Video.* Metuchen, N.J.: The Scarecrow Press, 1974.

MacBean, James R. *Film and Revolution.* Bloomington: Indiana University Press, 1975.

MacCann, Richard D., ed. *Film: A Montage of Theories.* New York: E. P. Dutton, 1966.

_____. *Film and Society.* New York: Charles Scribner's Sons, 1964.

Marcus, Fred H. *Film and Literature: Contrasts in Media.* Scranton, Pa.: Chandler, 1971.

Münsterberg, Hugo. *The Film: A Psychological Study.* New York: Dover, 1970 (originally published in 1916).

Murray, Edward. *The Cinematic Imagination.* New York: Ungar, 1974.

Ohrn, Stephen and Riley, Rebecca, eds. *Africa From Real to Reel: An African Filmography.* Waltham, Mass.: African Studies Association, 1976.

Powdermaker, Hortense. *Hollywood: The Dream Factory* (An Anthropologist Looks at Movie-Makers). Boston: Little, Brown, 1950.

Randall, Richard. *Censorship of the Movies.* Madison: University of Wisconsin Press, 1968.

Renan, Sheldon. *An Introduction to the American Underground Film.* New York: Oxford University Press, 1970.

Richards, Jeffrey. *Visions of Yesterday.* London: Routledge and Kegan Paul, 1973.

Richardson, Robert. *Literature and Film.* Bloomington: Indiana University Press, 1969.

Robinson, William R., ed. *Man and the Movies.* Baton Rouge: Louisiana State University Press, 1967.

Ross, T. J., ed. *Film and the Liberal Arts.* New York: Holt, Rinehart and Winston, 1970.

Rotha, Paul, et al. *The Documentary Film.* (3rd ed.) New York: Hastings, 1964.

Samples, Gordon. *How to Locate Reviews of Plays and Films.* Metuchen, N.J.: Scarecrow, 1976.

Sitney, P. A., ed. *Film Culture Reader.* New York: Praeger, 1970.

Sklar, Robert. *Movie-Made America: A Social History of American Movies.* New York: Random House, 1975.

Smith, Alfred, ed. *Communication and Culture.* New York: Holt, Rinehart and Winston, 1966.

Smith, Paul, ed. *The Historian and Film.* London: Cambridge University Press, 1976.

Snyder, Robert L. *Pare Lorentz and the Documentary Film.* Norman: University of Oklahoma Press, 1968.

Sohn, David. *Film: The Creative Eye.* Dayton, Ohio: Pflaum, 1970.

Starr, Cecile. *Discovering the Movies.* New York: Van Nostrand-Reinhold, 1972.

Suts, Lawrence. *Guts and Glory: Great American War Movies.* Reading, Mass.: Addison-Wesley, 1978.

Vogel, Amos. *Film as a Subversive Art.* New York: Random House, 1974.

Wagenknecht, Edward C. *The Movies in the Age of Innocence.* Norman: University of Oklahoma Press, 1962.

Warshow, Robert. *The Immediate Experience.* New York: Atheneum, 1970.

White, David M. and Averson, Richard. *The Celluloid Weapon: Social Comment in American Film.* Boston: Beacon Press, 1972.

_____. *Sight, Sound, and Society.* Boston: Beacon Press, 1968.

Wolfenstein, Martha and Leities, Nathan. *Movies: A Psychological Study.* New York: Free Press, 1950.

Wood, Michael. *America in the Movies.* New York: Basic Books, 1975.

MAJOR 16-MM FEATURE FILM DISTRIBUTORS

The following list is by no means exhaustive, but it does include most of the principal firms that rent feature movies for classroom use. The trend in the industry in recent years has been toward oligopoly as several large firms have been absorbing smaller competitors. That circumstance is likely to continue, and the economic impact on renters is not likely to be attractive.

Each of these distributors has a catalog, which will usually be provided free of charge on request. Asking for a catalog will also place one's name on mailing lists, and distributors will keep those people informed of the latest developments. Some update their catalog annually, whereas others do so at infrequent intervals. So long as inflation is a problem, price changes will often be made. and it is advisable before ordering to ascertain what the current rental fee is.

Any collection of distributors' catalogs will be enhanced and complemented by the purchase of three books:

Nadine Covert and Judith Trojan, compilers, *16 mm Film Distribution* (New York: Educational Film Library Association, 1977), $6.00.

James L. Limbacher, compiler, *Feature Films on 8 mm and 16 mm*, 5th ed. (New York: R. R. Bowker, 1977), $17.50.

Kathleen Weaver, compiler, *Film Programmers' Guide*

to 16 mm Rentals, 2nd ed. (Albany, Cal.: Reil Research, 1975), $10.00.

A.C.I. Films, 35 West Forty-fifth Street, New York, N.Y. 10036
Films, Inc., Chicago, Ill. 60604
Association-Sterling Films, Dept. AIM 866 Third Ave., New York, N.Y. 10022
Audio Ideal Pictures, 3910 Harlem Road, Buffalo, N.Y. 14226
Bailey Film Associates (BFA), 11559 Santa Monica Blvd., Los Angeles, Cal. 90025
Buchan Pictures, 122 W. Chippewa St., Jackson Bldg., Buffalo, N.Y. 14202
Budget Films, 4590 Santa Monica Blvd., Los Angeles, Cal. 90029
Carousel Films, 1501 Broadway, Suite 1503, New York, N.Y. 10036
Charard Motion Pictures, 2110 East Twenty-fourth St., Brooklyn, N.Y. 11229
Charlou Productions, Inc., 165 West Forty-sixth St., New York, N.Y. 10036
Churchill Films, 662 North Robertson Blvd., Los Angeles, Cal. 90069
Cine Craft Company, 1720 N.W. Marshall St., Portland, Ore. 97209
Cinema Center, P.O. Box 1569, Pittsfield, Mass. 01201
Cinema 5-16 mm, 595 Madison Ave., New York, N.Y. 10022
Classic Film Museum Inc., 4 Union Square, Dover-Foxcroft, Maine 04426
C.M.C. Films, 866 Third Avenue, New York, N.Y. 10022
Columbia Cinematheque, 711 Fifth Ave., New York, N.Y. 10022
Contemporary-McGraw-Hill Films, 1221 Avenue of the Americas, New York, N.Y. 10015
Em Gee Film Library, 16024 Ventura Blvd., Suite 211, Encino, Cal. 91436
The Film Center, 915 Twelfth Street N.W., Washington, D.C. 20005
Films Incorporated, 440 Park Avenue South, New York, N.Y. 10016
Genesis Films, 40 West Fifty-fifth Street, New York, N.Y. 10019
Samuel Goldwyn 16 mm, 1041 North Formosa Ave., Hollywood, Cal. 10046
Grove Press Films, 80 University Place, New York, N.Y. 10003
Hurlock Dine World Film Library, 230 West 41st St., New York, N.Y. 10036
Impact Films, 144 Bleeker Street, New York, N.Y. 10012
Institutional Cinema Service, 2323 Van Ness Avenue, San Francisco, Cal. 94109

International Film Bureau, 332 South Michigan Ave., Chicago, Ill. 60604

Janus Films, 745 Fifth Ave., New York, N.Y. 10022

Learning Corporation of America (Columbia Pictures), 711 Fifth Ave., New York, N.Y. 10022

Macmillan-Audio-Brandon Films, 34 Macquesten Parkway South, Mount Vernon, N.Y. 10550

Modern Sound Pictures, 1410 Howard St., Omaha, Neb. 68102

Mogull's Film Exchange, 235 West Forty-sixth St., New York, N.Y. 10036

Museum of Modern Art, Department of Film Circulating Programs, 11 West Fifty-third St., New York, N.Y. 10022

National Film Service, 14 Glenwood Ave., Raleigh, N.C. 27602

New Line Cinema, 121 University Place, New York, N.Y. 10003

New Yorker Films, 43 West Sixty-first Street, New York, N.Y. 10023

Newsreel, 322 Seventh Avenue, New York, N.Y. 10021

Pyramid Films, P.O. Box 1048, Santa Monica, Cal. 90406

Walter Reade Organ., 241 East Thirty-fourth Street, New York, N.Y. 10016

Roa's Films, 1696 North Astor St., Milwaukee, Wisc. 53202

Rogosin Films, Inc., 144 Bleeker St., New York, N.Y. 10012

Select Film Library, 115 West Thirty-first Street, New York, N.Y. 10001

Swank Motion Pictures, Inc., 201 South Jefferson, St. Louis, Mo. 63166

Thorne Films, 1229 University Avenue, Boulder, Colorado 80302

Time-Life Films, 43 West Sixteenth Street, New York, N.Y. 10011

Trans-World Films, 332 South Michigan Ave., Chicago, Ill. 60604

Tri-Continental Film Center, 333 Avenue of the Americas, New York, N.Y. 10014

Twyman Films, 329 Salem Avenue, Dayton, Ohio 45401

United Artists 16, 729 Seventh Avenue, New York, N.Y. 10019

United Films, 1425 South Main, Tulsa, Okla. 74119

United World Films, 221 Park Avenue South, New York, N.Y. 10003

Universal 16, 221 Park Avenue South, New York, N.Y. 10003

Warner Brothers 16, 666 Fifth Avenue, New York, N.Y. 10019

Westcoast Films, 25 Lusk Street, San Francisco, Cal. 94107

Wholesale Film Center, 20 Melrose St., Boston, Mass. 02116

Clem Williams Films, 2240 Noblestown Road, Pittsburgh, Pa. 15205

Willoughby-Peerless Film Exchange, 115 West Thirty-first St., New York, N.Y. 10017

Zipporah Films, 54 Lewis Wharf, Boston, Mass. 02110

INDEXES

MOVIES AND TELEVISION PROGRAMS

NAMES